BRITISH BALTIC TANKS

The Story of The Six Types of British 4 – 6 – 4 Tank Locomotives

C.E.J. Fryer

Published by Platform 5 Publishing Ltd., Wyvern House, Old Forge Business Park, Sark Road, Sheffield, S2 4HG, England.

Printed in England by Echo Press, Echo House, Jubilee Drive, Belton Park, Loughborough, Leics, LE11 OXS

ISBN 1872524 43 5

A superb photograph of Glasgow & South Western Railway 4 – 6 – 4 No. 545. Note the prominent bogie wheel guards, domed front to smokebox, circular hand-rail, planished steel boiler casing.

Mitchell Library Glasgow

CONTENTS

1. GENERAL DEVELOPMENT OF THE PASSENGER TANK LOCOMOTIVE 1830–1912

While over the years the British steam railway locomotive for the most part developed as a haulage machine attached to a separate tender that carried its supplies of fuel and water, another type of engine developed along with it in which containers to hold these necessities were fixed to its own frame. The first of the latter type that we know of was a contestant at the Rainhill trials of 1829, which were held to discover what might be the most suitable locomotive to haul goods and passenger traffic on the newly-built Liverpool and Manchester Railway. Braithwaite & Ericsson's *Novelty* may be regarded as the first tank engine. A line-diagram of it shows what is apparently a water tank combined with a coal bunker and furnace. Unsuccessful in the trials, *Novelty* was also well before its time; it was another seven years before a similar engine appeared.

A tank locomotive has two advantages over one which hauls a tender. Other things being equal, it is a lighter and shorter machine; also, when driven in reverse, it does not have to push an unwieldy tender before it. But there are also disadvantages. Carrying the water supply on the engine's main frame means, unless there is sufficient space under the coal bunker, that the tank or tanks must be awkwardly situated – especially in the case of well tanks beneath the boiler and between the framing which are difficult of access. If, instead of being placed there they are positioned over the boiler's top or along its sides, they have to be removed before the boiler can be got at for repairs or maintenance. A further disadvantage of the side tank type is that placing such a large dead weight of water on either side of the boiler makes the equilibrium less stable, so that the

One of the earliest tank engines to be built, for the broad gauge Bristol & Exeter Railway, in 1853. The driving wheels were 9 feet in diameter and had india rubber springs. Water was stored in a well tank.

Courtesy: National Railway Museum

engine is more liable to sway at speed – a fault which manifested itself more than once during the earlier years of the present century and was a contributory cause of the celebrated fatal railway accident at Sevenoaks in 1927 (see 'Railway Monographs No. 1 – The Rolling Rivers' by the same author).

After about the middle of the nineteenth century tank locomotives, whether of the well, saddle or side tank variety, began to multiply more rapidly in numbers. Without trying to comment on all the types which were built, one may mention a few of special significance or interest. The record for driving wheel diameter in any British locomotive was reached in two batches of 4 – 2 – 4 express tank engines built for the Bristol & Exeter Railway in 1853 and 1868. The earlier batch had enormous flangeless single driving wheels 9 feet in diameter, and all 10 wheels had indiarubber springing. They lasted for about 20 years. The second batch were similar in many respects, but had 8 ft. 10 in. driving wheels and plate springs instead of rubber ones. Both had well tanks and front and rear bogies whose pivots had no lateral play. After one of the latter type had suffered a derailment at speed the Great Western Railway (which by now had absorbed the BER and taken over its locomotive stock) converted the second batch into tender engines with 8 ft. driving wheels, and in this condition some of them lasted until the end of the broad gauge in 1892.

Between 1863 and 1875 Joseph Beattie, who had charge of the Locomotive Department on the London & South Western Railway, put as many as 85 2 – 4 – 0 tank engines on the road, which appeared to have coped very successfully with suburban traffic in the London area. Each one had two wells, under the footplate and between the frames over the leading axle, which was placed well behind the smokebox. They also had outside cylinders. In 1863 the first 2 – 4 – 2 tank engine appeared, built for the St. Helens Railway in Lancashire and named *The White Raven*. It had two interesting features – spring tyres and radial axleboxes for the front and rear carrying wheels. In the former steel hoop springs were interposed between the outer tyres and the iron wheel rims. The inventor of this device, William Adams, wished to introduce a measure of elasticity between tyre and wheel (such as there now is between the tread of an inflated pneumatic tyre and the wheel rim in a motor vehicle) but it does not appear to have been a successful gadget since *The White Raven* soon had its hoop springs removed and no other engines, so far as is known, were subsequently so fitted. The radial axleboxes were a different matter. These had curved guides which slid in curved grooves in the cheeks of the horn blocks so that the wheels could follow the line of the rails when these curved to one side or the other. The method proved successful and similar arrangements with the addition of controlling side springs, were soon widely used. This device, too, was Adams's invention.

The latter's inventive faculties were not exhausted since when he was Locomotive Superintendent on the North London Railway, he built, beginning in 1865, a number of 4 – 4 – 0 tank locomotives at the Company's Works in Bow which each had a lateral traverse for the bogie pivot, which moved to right or left in guides fixed in channel irons across the engine's frame. At first there were no side controls, but later on springs were added. Adams thus pioneered the way to the successful use of bogies on both tank and tender locomotives, which could not only support their front ends but also guide the driving wheels when rounding a curve, through the sideways pressure they imparted.

William Stroudley, Locomotive Superintendent on the London Brighton & South Coast Railway between 1870 and 1889, was the first engineer on a main railway system to go in for tank locomotives in a big way. In 1871 his celebrated 0 – 6 – 0 'Terriers' began to appear, whose coupled wheels were only 4 feet in diameter. They were originally intended for working trains over the South London line between Victoria and London Bridge, whose lightly-laid track would not support heavy machines, later they were widely used over the whole system. In 1873 Stroudley began to introduce his more numerous D Class 0 – 4 – 2 tanks, similar in appearance to the 'Terriers' but having larger coupled wheels, which also found work over the whole LBSCR system. Both types were tough and sturdy little engines; some of the Ds lasted until 1950, and there are a number of preserved 'Terriers' still to be seen on private lines here and there.

Other railways now began to develop 2 – 4 – 0 and 0 – 4 – 4 designs most of which, like Stroudley's engines, had inside cylinders, and all of which had side tanks with, in some cases, additional water space in wells between the axles or under the coal bunker.

Despite the tank engine's inherent drawbacks some were experimentally used on principal passenger trains by certain companies. The Lancashire & Yorkshire Railway built a number of 0 – 4 – 4s for use on its so-called 'expresses' on routes radiating from Manchester to Blackpool, Hellifield and Leeds. These were really not fast trains (the best start-to-stop speed was about 36 mph) and it is questionable whether the mile-a-minute rate ever needed to be attained. They were in fact only employed on these duties because of the difficulty of turning large tender engines, and once longer turntables had been installed 4 – 4 – 0s with tenders largely took their places.

One line which made good use of the 0 – 4 – 4 type was the Midland Railway, for which S.W. Johnson between 1875 and 1900 built some very graceful tank engines with this wheel arrangement, to a total of 205, for suburban work. Somewhat similar were the 0 – 4 – 4s constructed for the North Eastern Railway from 1874 onwards, with smallish cabs and (in the earlier batches) small side tanks, but really capacious coal

GER 2 – 4 – 2 tank No. 141 built 1864 by R. Sinclair. This engine had well tanks beneath the boiler and a boiler pressure of only 120 lbs per square inch.

Ken Nunn Collection.

bunkers. Almost all the 0 – 4 – 4s built during the period had inside cylinders, the only exceptions being four produced for the Caledonian Railway during 1873 – 1874, which had outside cylinders and coupled wheels of 4 ft 8 inch diameter spaced very closely together, so that there was a long gap between them and the rear bogie. Above the latter and behind a small cab was a combined bunker and water tank, there being no side tanks at all. These engines were used on the suburban services around Edinburgh and had very short lives.

The 2 – 4 – 2 type was particularly favoured at this time on the LNWR, for which F.W. Webb built 180 between 1879 and 1890. They had 4 ft. 7 in. coupled wheels, inside cylinders and Webb's patent radial axle-boxes for the leading and trailing carrying wheels, designed to ensure that the wheel bearings were approximately in line with the radius of any curve the engine was transversing. These locomotives were given, for their size, relatively large bunkers and side tanks, and were used for a while on the fast trains between Manchester and Leeds on the LNW route by way of Huddersfield, which was shorter but had steeper banks than the competing LYR route. Evidently they were not successful since they were soon taken off. The CR borrowed one to ascertain whether it might be a suitable design for use on the recently completed, heavily graded and sharply curved Callander & Oban Railway. On this line it performed well enough to mislead the CR into thinking that they could build some as good, but in this they failed, for so many derailments occurred that it became necessary for each engine to carry a re-railing device around with it. Eventually they were reconstructed and used elsewhere on the CR system.

Other lines preferred the 4 – 4 – 0 wheel arrangement. W. Adams, who had now moved to the LSWR, built for that railway several outside-cylindered tanks which were unusual in having solid disc bogie wheels only 2 ½ feet in diameter. These came out in 1878 – 1879 but they proved to have insufficient coal and water capacities, so he reconstructed them later as 4 – 4 – 2s with larger tanks and bunkers, which the addition of a trailing truck made possible. In 1880 the London Tilbury & Southend Railway began to build engines of this wheel arrangement which were termed 'universal', being intended for all types of traffic on this mainly passenger-carrying line. These too were able to hold

Above: MR 0 – 4 – 4 tank No. 1381 at Mill Hill, May 1909. Built 1878 by Johnson, rebuilt 1902.
Ken Nunn Collection

Right: 0 – 4 – 4 tank No. 349, built by J. Stirling during the 1880s, at the head of a local train at Faversham in September 1923. Not yet in SR livery.
SE&CR

respectable amounts of coal and water, and as long as the company continued its separate existence it relied on 4 – 4 – 2 tanks for its passenger haulage.

The 'eighties were a period when many locomotive engineers began to take an interest in compounding as a possible means of economising in fuel, and two in particular gave it an extensive trial, both with tender and tank locomotives. On the LNWR Webb produced four 3-cylinder compound tanks; the first (which was actually a reconstruction of a Beyer Peacock locomotive intended in its original form working in the tunnels of the Metropolitan Railway in London) being a 4 – 4 – 0 while the other three were 2 – 4 – 2s. Each had Webb's small outside high-pressure cylinders and an enormous inside low pressure one. One of these latter engines, announced with trumpets beforehand as a 'Patent Engine for Suburban Work', had, according to E.L. Ahrons,

.... not been in the London area a week before it had thoroughly earned the title. It was employed on the Broad Street and Mansion House service, and when making each of the many starts from the stations it indulged in and communicated to the train the peculiar fore-and-aft surging movement (*to which Webb's 3-cylinder compounds of all kinds were addicted*) to a superlative degree, thereby earning for itself more unpopularity with the travelling public than probably any locomotive ever built.

The trouble was that Webb refused, as with all his 3-cylinder compound passenger engines, to couple the driving wheels, so that the latter inevitably got out of phase. However, he did at length listen to reason (or bow to pressure) and scrap all his compound tanks during 1897 – 1901.

On the North Eastern Railway T.W. Worsdell in 1888

built a large number of $0-6-2$ tank locomotives on the von Borris 2-cylinder compound principle, in which one smaller high-pressure cylinder passes on its steam to one larger low-pressure cylinder before it is exhausted into the atmosphere. In Germany von Borries's engines, having outside cylinders of different sizes, looked peculiarly mis-shapen, but Wordsell placed both cylinders within the frames and managed to give his engines a more pleasing appearance, the asymmetry of the cylinders being out of sight. These tank engines were intended for short-haul freight working over the steeply-graded branch lines between the North Sea coast and the West Durham collieries, and seem to have carried out these duties efficiently enough as T.W. Wordsell's successor, his brother W. Wordsell, though he converted all the passenger compounds to simple-acting engines, did not similarly rebuild the goods engines.

During the later 'eighties and the 'nineties $2-4-2$ and $4-4-2$ tank types became more generally used, along with the $0-4-4$ variety, which was the most numerous of all, and smaller $2-4-0$s and $0-4-2$s of which the GWR built quite a number for use on its standard gauge sections. An accident in Cornwall called the use of front-coupled tanks travelling at speed into question. Two such engines heading a train became derailed, and the Inspector who inquired into the accident concluded that the track had been damaged by two similar engines which headed the train in front. This bought up the related questions of whether tank locomotives were less kind to the permanent way than tender engines, and whether the track in its turn, if not in good condition, was more unfriendly to tank engines than to those with tenders. Such considerations were to be very much in the forefront in the Inquiry into a later accident, the Sevenoaks derailment of 1927, which resulted in the complete reconstruction of all R.E.L. Maunsell's K Class $2-6-4$ tanks into tender locomotives.

By the end of the nineteenth century all lines in Great Britain were using tank engines for short-distance passenger and freight working and for shunting operations, and one of the smaller companies, the Wirral

Railway in Cheshire, was the first to put into service a twelve-wheeler, four-coupled with a four-wheel bogie at either end, thus foreshadowing the 14-wheelers with which this book principally deals. A larger $4-4-4$ was introduced in 1897 on the Midland & South Western Junction Railway, a cross-country line which straggled south-eastwards from Cheltenham through Gloucestershire, Wiltshire and Hampshire to connect with the LSWR at Andover. It traversed relatively dry limestone and chalk country so that an adequate tank capacity was important. The two that were built each had space for 1,900 gallons, just about enough for an end-to-end run of 70 miles with a fairly light train load.

The first 8-coupled tank locomotive appeared in 1896 when the Barry Railway in South Wales took delivery of seven $0-8-2$s for freight work. They had outside cylinders, 20 in. by 26 in. – the largest given to any tank locomotive up to that date – and enormous side tanks holding 2,100 gallons, which rose almost up to the level of the top of the boiler and extended forwards practical-

ly as far as the rear of the smokebox. The coupled wheels were only 4 ft. 3 in. in diameter. With a working pressure of 150 lb./sq. in. each could exert a tractive effort as the wheel rims of 26,000 lb, and with an adhesion weight of 62.8 tons there would be little chance of their slipping when it was applied. The drive was on the third pair of coupled wheels, whose tyres were given thinner flanges than those of the other coupled wheels for the better negotiation of curves. These engines were veritable monsters compared with other tank engines then running; however, the boiler, though long, was not of large diameter. Boilers wider than the gauge their engines ran on, which required chimneys and domes to be small and squat, were not produced until the following century.

However, the record for both size and for number of coupled wheels rested with the famous $0-10-0$ 'Decapod' built by James Holden of the Great Eastern Railway at the end of 1902. This engine was built to prove a point - that a suitably-designed steam locomotive could equal the accelerative capacity of a multiple-unit electric train and reach 30 m.p.h. in half a minute from rest with a 300 ton train. It had a boiler 5 ft. 2 in. in diameter, pressed to 200 lb./sq.in., a wide firebox similar to those later used on the GNR 'Atlantics', coupled wheels 4 ft 6 inches in diameter, and three cylinders with cranks set at 120 degrees. Water was contained in a well tank beneath the bunker, which held 1,500 gallons; above it was space for 2 tons of coal. In special trials on the main line near Chadwell Heath it proved its ability to accelerate at the required rate, but the Chief Engineer turned the design down because of its weight. So it was never used in daily service and Holden eventually rebuilt it as a freight locomotive with a tender and two fewer coupled wheels.

An accident at Llanelli, South Wales, in October 1904 caused a certain amount of public concern and for the second time brought into question the suitability of tank locomotives for working fast trains. A GWR express hauled by an inside-cylindered $4-4-0$ tender locomotive was being piloted over one part of its journey by an $0-6-0$ saddle-tank engine when it was derailed with considerable damage to the train; six passengers lost their lives and some 50 were injured. The railway journalist Charles Rous-Marten had some comments on the event in his monthly article in the *Railway Magazine* in April 1905:

Since the unfortunate mishap at Llanelly public attention has naturally been directed to tank engines and their suitableness for fast running. Authorities, engineering and otherwise, have had their say on this question and the result has been singularly indefinite. In effect they mostly say, 'We do not think tank engines so suitable as tender engines for express duty, but for the life of us we cannot tell *why* this should be the case.' .... My own opinion was sought on the point, and I ventured to suggest:-(1) That tank engines oscillate more than tender engines at *long-continued* high speed ..... owing to the absence of the corrective check applied by a tender with its large weight of 40 to 50 tons concentrated on a short wheel-base, and (2) that this tendency on

Left: L&SWR 0–4–4 Adams tank No. 1, at Bude, Cornwall, September 1923. Built 1894 and modified by Drummond with a more shapely chimney than the original Adams stovepipe.

Ken Nunn Collection

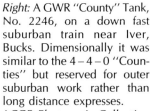

Right: A GWR "County" Tank, No. 2246, on a down fast suburban train near Iver, Bucks. Dimensionally it was similar to the 4–4–0 "Counties" but reserved for outer suburban work rather than long distance expresses.

LCGB Photomatic Collection

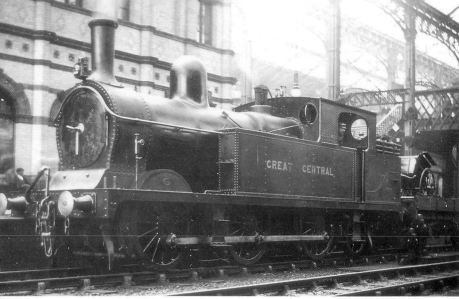

Left: GCR 0–6–2 tank No. 773 at Nottingham (Victoria), May 1901. Built by Pollitt, August 1898.

Ken Nunn Collection

Right: Class 13 4–4–2 tank locomotive No. 90 built in 1913 for the LB&SCR for express working. Seen here on the "Southern Belle" Pullman.

Author's Collection

Left: The experimental 0–10–0 tank locomotive built in 1902 by J. Holden for the GER. It was intended to demonstrate that a steam locomotive would accelerate as rapidly as an electric multiple unit. It did so, but was too heavy for the track and was rebuilt as a 0–8–0.

Ken Nunn Collection

the part of tank engines is cumulative when high speed is maintained for a considerable time and distance.

He then went on to enlarge on this problem, pointing out that if it were indeed true that speeds of from 50 to 60 miles per hour were dangerous when run by tank engines on expresses it ought to be just as dangerous to run fast with them on suburban trains, yet that was a matter of daily occurrence. He gave some examples of fast tank engine running on the suburban lines of the GWR and GNR – in the former case with speeds of up to 70 miles an hour. He speculated that the mishap might have something to do with the size of the driving wheels, but on the other hand admitted that much fast running was being done by locomotives with driving wheels only 5 ft in diameter, without adverse incident.

When all was said and done the GWR did not appear to have been deterred by what had happened at Llanelli, since the following year Swindon Works began to produce a class of passenger tank locomotives whose main dimensions were identical with those of the 4 – 4 – 0 express passenger 'Counties' that had preceded them.

Thirty were built. Like their tender-attached fellows they had coned boilers pressed to 200 lb./sq.in. outside cylinders 18 in. by 30 in. and driving wheels 6 ft 8 in. in diameter - the largest ever given up to that time to a tank engine since the Bristol & Exeter 4 – 2 – 4s mentioned above. Like the 'Counties' these were intended for use on fast trains, though not on long distance expresses, and had two-way water scoops fixed (though these were later removed). They were eventually employed on outer residential trains from and to Paddington, some of which had non-stop schedules between there and Reading of 40 or 41 minutes, which certainly required mile-a-minute running. None of them was ever involved in any accident which caused loss of life or injury.

The following year George Whale, F.W. Webb's successor on the LNWR began to produce his 4 – 4 – 2 'Precursor Tanks'. These, like the GWR 'County' tanks were a version of a 4 – 4 – 0 express locomotive type, the 'Precursors', first built in 1904. They had a lower boiler pressure than the 'County' tanks, and inside cylinders, and their coupled wheels were 6 inches smaller. They were used on semi-fast and outer suburban trains, and also for piloting or pushing expresses up the Grayrigg and Shap inclines. They, too, had an accident-free record.

But it was one of the smaller British companies which pioneered the use of the tank locomotive on principal expresses. The LBSCR had no through passenger trains which travelled further than from Victoria to Portsmouth, 86 miles by way of Horsham and Chichester, and no non-stop journeys exceeding 51 miles, so it was well placed to exploit the double advantage of lesser weight and shorter length, other things being equal, over the tender locomotive. D.E. Marsh, who succeeded R.J. Billinton as Locomotive Superintendent at Brighton in January 1905, first introduced the 4 – 4 – 2 tank type in 1906 with his 'I1' and followed them with the slightly larger 'I2' in 1907. Both types turned out to be disappointingly poor steamers. Later in 1907, however, he built his first 'I3' tank with 6 ft. 9 in. wheels, and the following year added to it several others, giving them slightly smaller driving wheels and superheaters. They

were a striking success, coping with the Company's best expresses while at the same time using much less coal and water. To cope with increasing train loads Marsh in his last year at Brighton also built two more passenger tank engines with six-coupled driving wheels as an experiment, and they too were highly successful. The story of these Brighton tank locomotives and how they achieved more than local fame is set out at the beginning of Chapter 3 below.

One may finally notice the 'Coronation' 4 – 6 – 2 tank engines of the Great Central Railway, designed by J.G. Robinson in 1910, which began to appear the following year. Like all the Robinson's designs they were extremely handsome machines, with inside cylinders 20 in. by 26 in.; they were the first GCR engines to be built with superheaters; their tanks held 2,280 gallons of water and their bunkers just over 4 tons of coal. Their coupled wheels were only 5 ft. 7 inches in diameter, but this did not prevent them from running fast when necessary. They were initially put on the Marylebone – Aylesbury and Marylebone – High Wycombe Services, and some of the schedules to which they had to adhere were quite fast, such as 29 minutes for the 21 miles from Aylesbury to Rickmansworth over the steep banks of the Metropolitan Extension after the First World War, and following the absorption of the GCR into the London & North Eastern Railway the latter's Chief Mechanical Engineer, H.N. Gresley, had yet more constructed, bringing the total to 45. They were still on front-line duty in BR days, then known as Class A5, being used to take over from electric traction at Guide Bridge on Hull – Liverpool expresses for the short section to Manchester Central.

With the latter engines it might appear that the tank engine had reached its limit in size, but some locomotive engineers already had it in mind to build larger ones, and Robinson himself had pondered on whether to make his 4 – 6 – 2 a 4 – 6 – 4, and drawings for the latter had been tentatively prepared. On one of the smaller British lines the decision had already been taken, and the order for building the first British 'Baltic' type of tank locomotive was about to be placed.

Ex-GCR 4 – 6 – 2 tank No. 69806 leaving Marylebone on 7th May 1949 with a football special for Wembley.
Ken Nunn Collection

PLATFORM 5 PUBLISHING LIMITED
COMPLETE TRADE BOOK LIST

Wyvern House, Old Forge Business Park, Sark Road, SHEFFIELD, S2 4HG.

NEW TITLES   Price

1 872524 49 3	British Railways Locomotives & Coaching Stock 1993	7.25
1 872524 50 8	German Railways Locomotives & MUs 3rd edition *END APRIL*	12.50
1 872524 51 6	Manx Electric **END APRIL**	7.95
1 872524 40 0	6203 'Princess Margaret Rose'	19.95
1 872524 43 5	British Baltic Tanks	6.95
1 872524 44 3	Light Rail Review 4 **MARCH 20th**	7.50
0 900609 95 8	British Rail Track Diagrams 1 — Scotland & Isle of Man (Quail)	5.00
1 870119 20 7	Scenes from the Past 16 — Midland from Manchester (Foxline)	9.95
0 946265	Bus Review 8 (Bus Enthusiast) **MARCH**	4.95

Modern British Railway Titles

1 872524 45 1	Motive Power Pocket Book Spring 1993	1.80
1 872524 46 X	Coaching Stock Pocket Book 1993	1.80
1 872524 47 8	Diesel Unit Pocket Book 1993	1.80
1 872524 48 6	Electric Unit Pocket Book 1993	1.80
1 872524 27 3	Preserved Locomotives of British Railways 7th Edition	5.50
0 906579 97 X	Departmental Coaching Stock 4th Edition	4.95
1 872524 22 2	On-Track Plant on British Railways 4th Edition	5.50
1 872524 38 9	The Fifty 50s in Colour	5.95
1 872768 09 1	British Rail Internal Users (SCTP)	7.95
1 872768 08 3	British Rail Wagon Fleet—Air Braked Freight Stock (SCTP)	6.95
1 872768 07 5	RIV Wagon Fleet (SCTP)	5.95
0 9509354 2 5	Blood, Sweat and Fifties (Fearless)	4.95
0 947796 13 4	Miles & Chains Volume 2 — London Midland (Milepost)	1.40
0 947796 10 X	Miles & Chains Volume 3 — Scottish (Milepost)	1.00
0 947796 08 8	Miles & Chains Volume 5 — Southern (Milepost)	1.00

Overseas Railways

1 872524 09 5	Swiss Railways/Chemins de Fer Suisses	9.95
1 872524 25 7	French Railways/Chemins de Fer Francais	9.95
0 906579 87 2	ÖBB/Austrian Federal Railways 2nd Edition	6.95
0 906579 96 1	Benelux Locomotives & Coaching Stock 2nd Edition	6.95
0 9509354 1 7	A Guide to Portuguese Railways (Fearless)	4.95
0 620166 88 6	Southern Africa Locomotive Guide 1992 (Beyer—Garratt)	4.00
	Canadian Trackside Guide 1990 (Including Preserved)	9.95

Historical Railway Titles

0 906579 72 4	Midland Railway Portrait	12.95
1 872524 16 8	Steam Days on BR 1 — The Midland Line in Sheffield	4.95
1 872524 15 X	Rails along the Sea Wall (Dawlish—Teignmouth Pictorial History)	4.95
1 872524 39 7	The Rolling Rivers	6.95
0 906579 71 6	The Railways of Winchester	6.95
0 947796 18 5	Register of Closed Railways 1948—1991 (Milepost)	5.95
0 86093 206 0	Private Owner Wagons Volume 3 (Headstock)	6.95
0 9512793 0 0	Private Owner Wagons Volume 4 (Headstock)	7.95
0 9520168 0 X	Scottish Colliery Pugs in the Seventies (Robertson)	4.95

Rambling

0 906579 86 4	Rambles by Rail 1 — The Hope Valley Line	1.95
1 872524 17 6	Rambles by Rail 2 — Liskeard—Looe	1.95
0 9511353 0 9	Buxton Spa Line Rail Rambles	1.20

Political **Price**

1 872524 07 9 The Battle for the Settle & Carlisle............................ 6.95

Light Rail Transit, Trams, Buses, Ships & Aircraft

1 872524 00 1 Light Rail Review 1 .... 6.95
1 872524 23 0 Light Rail Review 2 .... 7.50
1 872524 30 3 Light Rail Review 3 .... 7.50
1 872524 36 2 UK Light Rail Systems No.1: Manchester Metrolink................ 8.50
0 906579 83 X Blackpool & Fleetwood By Tram................................. 7.50
1 870119 09 6 Tramways in and around Stockport (Foxline)..................... 6.95
1 870119 12 6 Glossop Tramways (Foxline).................................... 4.50
0 946265 15 1 London Buses in Exile 2nd Edition (Bus Enthusiast)................ 4.95
0 946265 09 7 Edinburgh's Trams & Buses (Bus Enthusiast)..................... 4.95
0 946265 16 X Sixty Years of A1 Service (Bus Enthusiast)..................... 5.95
0 946265 13 5 Speed Bonny Boat (Bus Enthusiast)............................ 4.95
0 9512793 3 5 Tramtracks & Trolleybooms (Headstock)......................... 3.95
               Plastic Kit Constructor 32 (Aircraft Modelling Magazine)............ 2.95
               Flying Model Designer & Constructor 3 (Flying Model Magazine).... 1.50

Scenes from the Past (Foxline Publishing)

1 870119 05 3 Scenes from the Past 6 − Preston REPRINT..................... 6.95
1 870119 06 1 Scenes from the Past 7 − Buxton/Ambergate REPRINT........... 6.95
1 870119 13 4 Scenes from the Past 11 − Railways around Nottingham.......... 8.95
1 870119 14 2 Scenes from the Past 12 − The Conwy Valley.................. 7.95
1 870119 17 7 Scenes from the Past 13 − Stockport Tiviot Dale.............. 5.95
1 870119 18 5 Scenes from the Past 14 − Bangor........................... 7.95
1 870119 19 3 Scenes from the Past 15 − Denbigh/Mold Line (Foxline).......... 9.95

Maps & Track Diagrams (Quail Map Company)

0 900609 84 2 British Rail Track Diagrams 3 − Western....................... 5.00
0 900609 74 5 British Rail Track Diagrams 4 − London Midland................. 6.95
0 900609 69 9 London Railway Map.. 5.95
0 900609 80 X London Transport Track Map.................................... 1.30
0 900609 93 1 Czech Republic & Slovakia Railway Map........................ 1.70
0 900609 89 3 Poland Railway Map.. 2.00

PVC Book Covers

               A6 Pocket Book Covers (pack of 25 in assorted colours)............. 20.00
NEW   Locos & Coaching Stock Covers (pack of 25 in assorted colours)..... 25.00
NEW   A5 Book Covers (pack of 12 in assorted colours)................... 16.80

Reduced Price Titles

               The Handbook of British Railways Steam Motive Power Depots
0 906579 99 6 Volume 1 − Southern England (was 7.95)........................ 3.95
0 906579 95 3 Volume 2 − Central England, East Anglia & Wales (was 8.95)...... 3.95
1 872524 04 2 Volume 3 − North Midlands, Lancashire & Yorkshire (was 8.95).... 3.95
1 872524 15 1 Volume 4 − Northern England & Scotland (was 9.95)............. 3.95
1 872524 35 4 North West Rails in Colour (was 8.50)......................... 4.25
0 906883 09 1 In Memory of the Forties (Rail Photoprints)..................... 2.95
0 906883 07 5 Portrait of the Fifties (Rail Photoprints)....................... 2.95

Discount of 33.33% will be given on trade orders, but please note: Orders with a total retail value of less than £10 can only be supplied on a cash with order basis and must be accompanied by contribution to postage of 10% of retail value (20% overseas).

We can only accept cheques payable in POUNDS STERLING or US Dollar cheques if the equivalent of £3.00 is added to cover currency conversion.

For further information about any of the above titles, please contact our trade sales department at the above address, or by telephone on 0742-552625. Fax: 0742-552471.

2. WHITELEGG'S BALTICS FOR THE SOUTHEND LINE

In a well-known Victorian music-hall song, a young woman complains that she took her harp to a party but nobody asked her to play. Something analogous happened to the first batch of 4 – 6 – 4 tank locomotives built for service on a British railway. The sort of tune it might have produced was never really discovered, and the magnificent appearance it might have displayed, had it been liveried as its designer intended, can now only be appreciated by viewing a model in a museum.

The London Tilbury and Southend Railway occupied an unusual position among the smaller British lines, its nearest analogue being the North London Railway, which also had its main terminus in the City of London, traversed suburban areas and put out some short branch lines; it, too, used tank locomotives for all its trains and was also mainly a passenger line, and a commuters' line in particular. But there were differences. Whereas the NLR served the inner Northern and Western suburbs of London, and had a main route only 16 ¼ miles long from Broad Street to Richmond, the LTSR served the region east of London and north of the Thames estuary, and extended over twice as far to reach Southend-on-Sea and Shoeburyness; the latter, the line's Eastern extermity, being almost forty miles from Fenchurch Street terminus. The branches, too, were longer, one in fact being a loop by way of Tilbury along which some Southend-bound trains travelled. Much of the LTSR route passed through what was then open country, Tilbury and Southend being the only large towns which it served East of Barking. Also, whereas the NLR's trains halted at all stations, which were never more than a mile

Below: LT&SR 4 – 4 – 2 tank No. 38, "Westcliff", waiting to back on to a Southend train at Fenchurch Street. Built in 1897. Seen here in 1909.   *Ken Nunn Collection*

and a half apart and in most places much closer, so that rapid running was impossible, the LTSR on the other hand had a number of services which omitted several stops, and some commuter trains which could almost rank as expresses, such as the evening business train which was booked to cover the 36 ¼ miles from Fenchurch Street to Westhill-on-sea in 47 minutes, the first few miles having to be covered at a restricted speed. So the locomotives needed to be capable of sprightly running and, when employed on stopping trains, of rapid acceleration.

Until 1880 the LTSR was under Great Eastern management, and it was W. Adams, then Locomotive Superintendent on the latter line, who established the tradition of building 4 – 4 – 2 tank engines with outside cylinders to do all the haulage work on the line - mostly of passenger trains, though some freight trains also had to be taken to and from Tilbury Docks. After the line became a completely independent concern in 1880 Thomas Whitelegg succeeded Adams and held the locomotive superintendency at Plaistow works for 31 years. He continued Adams' policy putting out successive designs of 4 – 4 – 2 tanks, each larger and more powerful that its predecessor, to cope with increasing loads. These in Adams' time had usually been trains of 9 four-wheelers, but by 1910 they had increased to about 13 eight-wheelers. In the year before Whitelegg's retirement his latest design came into service; it was a massive engine whose adhesion-weight on its 4-coupled wheels was officially some 40 tons and may well have been more. One of these locomotives, No. 80, *Thundersley*, has been preserved at Bressingham Live Steam Museum, Norfolk, repainted in its former green livery with red frames and edging and black-and-white lining out, to show how smart it would have looked when it first took the rails. These engines could just about cope with the system's heaviest trains in the last few years of the Company's independent existence, but something larger now seemed to be called for, with a reserve of power.

Whitelegg's son, Robert, succeeded his father on the latter's retirement in 1910, after having been his Chief Assistant for the previous ten years. He had evidently been meditating on the provision of a batch of larger six-coupled locomotives for some time, as within two months of his appointment he had set his design team to work on the project, and had prepared an outline of a new proposed engine. This would have been a 4 – 6 – 4 using saturated steam at 200 lb./sq.in. and having driving wheels of only 5 ft. 9 in. diameter, which indicated that rapid starts rather than sustained high speeds was the chief *desideratum*. But even as the design took shape amendments suggested themselves in par-

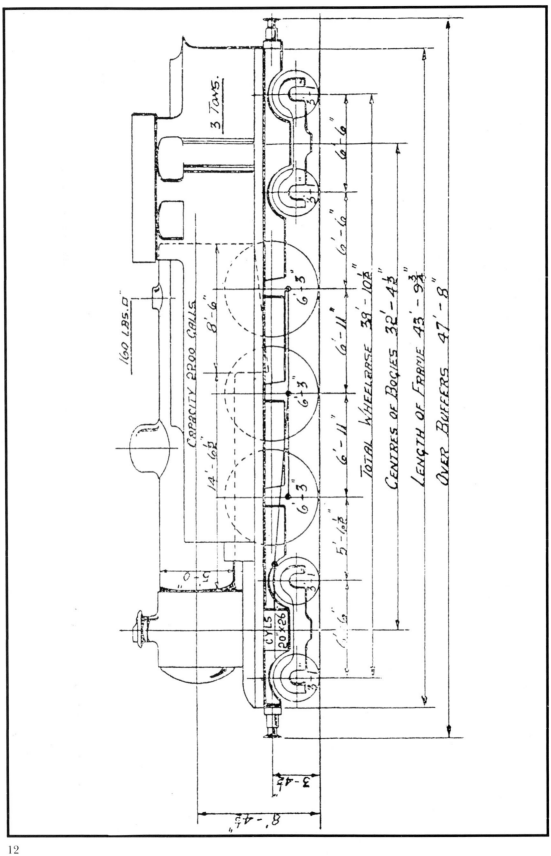

WHITELEGG 2 CYLINDER 4-6-4T BUILT AT BEYER PEACOCK IN 1912 FOR THE LONDON TILBURY & SOUTHEND RAILWAY

Above: The driver (with oilcan), fireman and a stationmaster pose beside No. 2104 at the head of a train somewhere on the Southend line. Note the projecting front wheel guards, laterally-arranged safety valves and bogie wheel splashers; also the bulging smokebox door, a feature that re-appeared on his later G&SWR 'Baltics'

P.J. Hughes Collection

Below: No. 2100, the first of the LT&SR 'Baltics' at Plaistow. Note the formal attire with high-cut jacket of the gentleman (a foreman?) on the buffer beam.

National Railway Museum

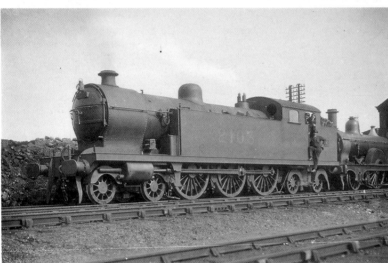

Above: No. 2101 in photographic grey posed for the official picture. Note the MR coat of arms beneath the cab window and the maker's plate on the side of the bunker.　*National Railway Museum*

Left: No. 2103, shorn of tank-top tool chests and with MR-type chimney, in MR livery standing in front of a Johnson 2 – 4 – 0.
　Locomotive Publishing Company

Left: No. 2105 in the paint shop at Derby. Toolbox not yet removed but MR-style smokebox door fitted.
　C.J. Fryer Collection

ticular the addition of superheating, which was already proving itself to be a fuel saver with the 'I3' 4 – 4 – 2 tanks of the LBSCR and the newly-built 'George the Fifth' Class of the LNWR. Accordingly it was decided to install a superheater. At the same time the proposed diameter of the coupled wheels was increased to 6 ft. 3 in.

The modified design was finished and approved by Robert Whitelegg. As completed it had a number of unusual features. The provision of a superheater was used as an opportunity for lowering the boiler pressure so that the boiler drums, firetubes, smokebox and firebox tube plates could be made of thinner metal, Whitelegg being particularly concerned that the engine should not be too heavy. (This thinning of material was to have the unfortunate result that leaks developed at the ends of the tubes, a trouble that was not cured until the MR authorities took the engines in hand and rebuilt them at Derby in 1916/1917 with thicker plates and tubes. The superheater was one of the Schmidt pattern with 18 elements, and provided moderately high superheat. The smokebox had a sloping floor with an ash chute that could be opened and shut from the footplate when the engine was in motion. Steam was admitted to the cylinders by piston valves 10 inches in diameter, operated by Stephenson valve gear between the frames; the lap of 1 inch and maximum travel of 4½ inches showed that the long-lap, long-travel revolution begun at Swindon under Churchward had not yet reached Plaistow. The cylinders had prominent tail rods, and the connecting rods from the crossheads to the middle coupled wheels were, at 11 ft. 7 in. longer than any other British locomotive. The valve gear was linked to a device for varying the blast-pipe orifice so that, whatever the cut-off might be, the draught would be uniform.

The frames, in an engine which had not to be excessively heavy, were unusually massive, the plating being 1¼ inches thick. The cab was provided with side windows and was unusually roomy; a Westinghouse pump was installed within it. Above the tanks on either side were long compartments for the fire-irons. Most unusually, the coal bunker had hinged lids; these, however, were later taken away to make more room for coal, the 3 tons' capacity being too small to allow for runs of the length that the MR authorities had in mind.

In order to determine whether the engine would be able to negotiate curves of the minimum radius on the line, Whitelegg had a model of the frame and wheels built, and wheeled over track laid down to the appropriate scale. This was later completed with a facsimile superstructure with all the external features faithfully reproduced and carefully painted in the intended manner, even down to the cooper rim on the flared chimney. It was also given a name, *Arthur Lewis Stride*, that of the system's General Manager. The model became Whitelegg's personal property and was eventually bequethed to the Science Museum in South Kensington.

Had these engines ever been completed in the livery shown on the model they would have been ornate and magnificent objects, outshining in their chromatic glory all other tank locomotives in the country. But this never happened, for while Beyer Peacock & Co. of Manchester

were in process of manufacturing the eight locomotives that the LTSR ordered, this railway was sold, lock, stock and barrel, to the Midland Railway and ceased to exist as an independent concern. Robert Whitelegg, not unnaturally dis-satisfied with having to take a subordinate position, eventually resigned, and for a while left railway work altogether. Before doing so, however, he tried out each engine as it was delivered.

On one of these trials No. 2104 (in MR numbering, for these engines never carried out their intended LTSR numbers) was said to have reached a maximum speed of 94 m.p.h. on the level or gently downhill stretch between Upminster and Barking, a quite astonishing feat with a locomotive lacking the sophisticated front end design which had not yet spread much beyond Swindon, and whose driving wheels were only 6 ft. 3 in. in diameter. Not that the latter fact would necessarily inhibit high speed; it certainly did not do so in Bulleid's 'Merchant Navy' and 'West Country' Pacifics built 30 years later, of which types 3-figure maxima have been recorded. The absence of long valve travel would have been a more serious handicap. However, *City of Truro* achieved its 100 m.p.h. record maximum without piston valves or long valve-travel, so one need not write off No. 2104's alleged achievement as impossible. It may well have been an all-time record for a tank engine of any type, and one doubts whether any of the class at a later date ever had the chance to exceed 80, let alone 90.

The MR authorities did not really know what to do with these new monsters. In fact, at first nobody knew. They had been built with a large axle load on each of the coupled wheels, and Whitelegg himself had been in some doubt whether they might not be too heavy for the LTSR track. However, A.L. Stride, the General Manager, told him to go ahead - and he had previously been the line's Civil Engineer and presumably knew what the track would carry. But further inspection while the locomotives were being delivered showed that there were underline bridges between Barking and Fenchurch Street which could not safely take the weight of the new type. For them to have been used on the principal trains it would have been necessary to change engines at Barking, which would have added some minutes to the scheduled times. On such a booking as the 47-minute run from Fenchurch Street to Westcliff-on-Sea it would not have been possible to absorb this delay.

In any case the MR authorities had no use for six-coupled passenger engines. On their own system all the latter were 4 – 4 – 0s, and the weights of trains were kept down to what they could haul. So it was decided to dispose of the 'Baltics', selling the whole batch to any line or lines that would buy them, at a cut price some 80 per cent of what the makers had charged. As early as the spring of 1913 two of them were run over MR metals to Temple Meads station, Bristol, and handed over to the GWR, who tried them out for a short period before returning one of them to the MR and passing the other, No. 2107, to the South Eastern & Chatham Railway, handing it over at Reading, that line's westernmost extremity.

On the SECR the engine was tested out, first between Reading and Redhill by way of Guildford and Dorking,

Left: No. 2107 at Plaistow, with MR-style smokebox door and Ramsbottom safety valves arranged longitudinally; tool chests not yet removed from tank tops, but cover removed from bumker top.

Photomatic

Left: No. 2196 leaving Radlett on a St. Albans – London St. Pancras train, June 1928. Renumbered from 2104. This engine was reported to have attained 94 m.p.h. near Up-minster soon after being built.

LCGB Ken Nunn Collection

Right: No. 2196 at the head of a local train about to leave London St. Pancras.

Photomatic

Left: No. 2198, formerly 2106 in LMS livery.

C.J. Fryer Collection

and then between Redhill and Cannon Street by way of Croydon. The results seem to have persuaded the SECR Board that it would be a good idea to acquire all eight. Wainwright, that Railway's Locomotive Superintendent, and Surtees, his Chief Draughtsman, were less enthusiastic. Some tests were arranged on the straight section between Ashford and Tonbridge, to assess the locomotive's speed potential and haulage ability, Wainwright and Surtees both being on the footplate. It appears that the latter found fault with its tendency to roll - though a section more free from curvature it would have been hard to find in Britain, apart from the Darlington-York stretch of the North Eastern Railway. Bearing in mind the vicissitudes of the K Class 2 – 6 – 4 tank locomotives built later by R.E.L. Maunsell for the Eastern Section of the Southern Railway, which were also accused of rolling, and of the findings of the Inquiry into the accident in which one of them was involved at Sevenoaks, one may wonder whether the condition of the track-bed may have been the main reason why the 'Baltic' proved unsteady. Both men also felt that the water and coal capacities of this engine was insufficient and recommended that the MR's offer be declined.

The latter company was therefore obliged to find some use for them, and for a while they were employed on the line for which they had been designed, working between Shoeburyness and Barking on through trains to Ealing by way of the London District and Metropolitan systems, and then on similar trains to St. Pancras by way of Barking and Kentish Town. Eventually they were taken away from the LTSR system altogether and used on outer suburban services between St. Pancras and Luton. During the First World War they were taken off passenger work and used to haul coal trains between Wellingborough and Brent sidings; on these duties, since the trains were very heavy, they were frequently piloted by a smaller locomotive, which on occasion might be a Johnson 4 – 2 – 2 in the evening of its days. After the War had ended they went back to Plaistow and worked to and from St. Pancras. Occasionally one might stray into other pastures further North, especially after repair at Derby or (later) at Crewe.

The MR authorities did not allow them to remain long in their designed condition. The flared chimneys with their copper tops were soon replaced by the standard MR variety. The distinctive smokebox doors, dished and provided with hand-rails which curved above them, gave place to Derby-pattern types. The long boxes for holding the fire-irons above the side tanks were removed. The Westinghouse pumps, which had been fixed inside the cabs, so that the latter became very hot in the summer weather, were removed and the vacuum-braking system was fitted instead. The first of the type had its Schmidt superheater removed in September 1914; it was soon found that this was no improvement since coal and water consumption at once showed an increase. Under Midland ownership all eight engines were painted red. After the MR had been absorbed into the London Midland and Scottish railway they were painted in black as they came in for re-conditioning.

It is impossible to guess how these engines would have coped with the main services between London and Southend for which they have been designed. No records ever seem to have been made of their work. Their lives were short and uneventful, the first to be withdrawn being scrapped in February 1929; the last survived until 1934. Only the gorgeous wooden model in the Science Museum at South Kensington remains to testify to the genius of its designer.

3. BILLINTON'S BALTICS FOR THE BRIGHTON LINE

The LBSCR was the smallest of the eleven larger English railway companies so far as track mileage was concerned and had no through services longer than those covering the 87 miles between Victoria and Portsmouth. It was therefore a system which could operate all its passenger trains by means of tank locomotives if its management chose to do so. During the last years of its separate existence it began to look as if this might eventually happen.

The last tender-attached type designed for express passenger work on the Brighton line was Earle Marsh's 'Atlantic', modelled on the large-boilered 4 – 4 – 2 built by H.A. Ivatt for the Great Northern Railway. Five were constructed in 1905/1906 and six more were added later, some alterations being made, including the provision of superheating. As early as 1906, however, Marsh signalled a change of intention when he built his 'I1' class of 4 – 4 – 2 passenger tank engines for semi-fast duties, 20 appearing in that year, and followed these in 1907 with 10 'I2' that had slightly larger boilers and extended smokeboxes. Neither of these types came up to expectations, proving poor steamers. But even before the last one had emerged from Brighton Works a third version had appeared, the 'I3'. The prototype was built as a tank engine based upon R.J. Billinton's 'B4' 4 – 4 – 0 tender locomotives; it had 6 ft. 9 in. wheels and was intended for use with express passenger trains. When it had been completed, in the course of discussion with his Chief Draughtsman B.K. Field, Marsh accepted the latter's suggestion that the 'I3's which followed the prototype should be re-styled in appearance so that they did not look as if Billinton had been responsible for them, and that some should be fitted with superheaters. This was done, and once they had been constructed the superheated 'I3's showed themselves to be markedly lighter on coal and water than their non-superheated fellows, and were able to cope with such services as the afternoon Portsmouth express which ran non-stop between Clapham Junction and Fratton, 84 miles, with a light train but over a heavily-graded road, without having to halt to refill their tanks.

The stage was now set for the gradual replacement of tender engines by tank engines on fast passenger duties, and a striking confirmation that this could be successfully achieved came during November 1909, when for a while the 'Sunny South Express' from Liverpool and Manchester to Brighton, formerly hauled by an LNWR engine as far as Willesden Junction (where an direction) was handed over at Rugby instead. An 'I3' tank, No. 23, ran turn and turn about with an LNWR 'Precursor' 4 – 4 – 0 No. 7 *Titan* and showed it could keep time with the 250-ton train between Croydon and Rugby

by way of Clapham Junction and Kensington, 90 ½ miles, without needing to stop for water. (It had no water-scoop and so could not, like the 'Precursor', use the troughs at Bushey and Castlethorpe). Furthermore, it could make the double journey from Brighton to Rugby and back, over 260 miles, on a single bunker-ful of coal.

Marsh retired in 1911, but before going he superintended the design of the two 4 – 6 – 2 tank engines which together formed class J. These were in effect superheated 'I3', with an extra pair of coupled wheels, larger boilers and rather more capacious bunkers and water tanks and outside cylinders, the first, No. 325, *Abergavenny*, had a water capacity of 2,300 gallons and inside Stephenson valve gear; the second, No. 326, *Bessborough*, had rather smaller tanks and outside Walschaert's valve gear. The two engines were put on to the London to Brighton main line services as soon as they had been run in, and worked the fast 60-minute non-stop trains, including the all-Pullman 'Southern Belle', successfully.

Marsh was succeeded as Locomotive Superintendent by L. Billinton, the son of R.J. Billinton. His first express locomotive design was a tank engine even larger than the two 4 – 6 – 2s, though as will be seen he seemed to have had some reservations, as to whether a tender-attached 4 – 6 – 0 might not be a preferable solution to the problem of providing greater locomotive power. Loads were increasing yearly, and the two six-coupled tanks and Marsh Atlantics, of which there were now 11, were found to be only just adequate for timekeeping when circumstances were adverse, as in winter when bad weather and the need to supply steam for heating the train as well as for hauling it added to the difficulties experienced through signal and other delays. With a tender locomotive, though it would weigh up to 20 tons heavier than an equally powerful tank engine, one could at least be assured of an adequate water supply, positioned where it did not affect the locomotive's equilibrium.

Billinton therefore went ahead with the design and construction of a 4 – 6 – 4 tank locomotive which was to be larger in every respect than the two 4 – 6 – 2s, but he hedged his bets by at the same time beginning the assembly of a 4 – 6 – 0 express engine intended to be of similar dimensions to the 4 – 6 – 4 in boiler, cylinders and machinery. It looked as though he meant to compare the two and see which was the most satisfactory in traffic.

The new 4 – 6 – 4 was completed in March 1914 and began its trials. Numbered 327 and named *Charles C Macrae* after one of the directors, it was a most handsome machine, with cylinders larger than had ever been used by the Company before and piston valves operated by Walschaert's valve gear, which was fixed externally

Above: 'J' Class 4 – 6 – 2 tank locomotive No. 326, *Bessborough*, at Victoria, D.E. Marsh's latest design for working the London to Brighton 60 minute services.   *L.C.G.B. Photomatic Collection*

Below: The first LB&SCR 'Baltic' as originally built before the installation of well tanks, posed for the official photograph.   *National Railway Museum*

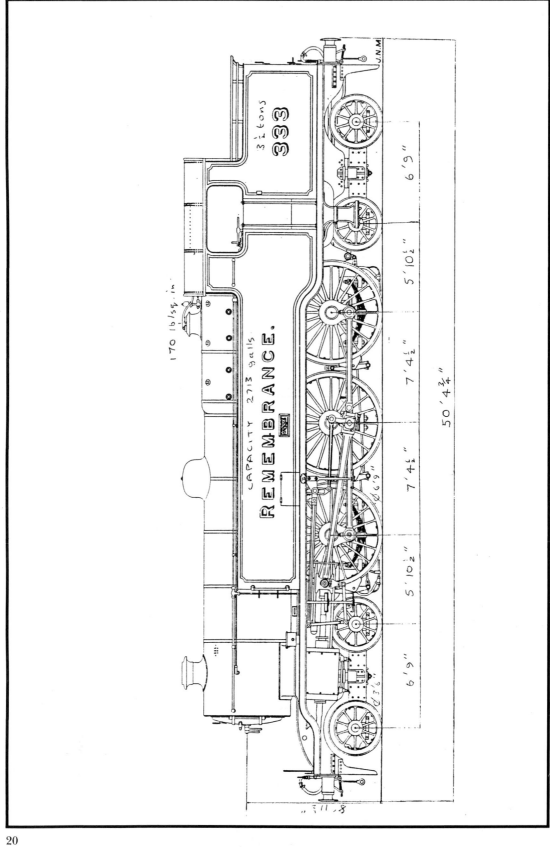

BILLINTON'S 2 CYLINDER BALTIC DESIGN FOR THE LONDON BRIGHTON & SOUTH COAST RAILWAY

but worked on valves that were between, not above the cylinders, and which received their movements indirectly through rocking levers. The large size of the cylinders was to make possible rapid acceleration from rest and the quick climbing of gradients, features which the locomotive and its later-built companions were certainly able to demonstrate. The boiler was of large diameter and had two parallel rings; its working pressure at 170 lb./sq.in. was a little on the low side; it had a Belpaire firebox (the first example of its use on a passenger express engine by this company) and an extended smokebox holding a Robinson type of superheater with 27 elements and an exceptionally large heating surface. The bunker was capacious enough to enable non-stop runs to be made from Victoria to Portsmouth (though this was never in fact attempted) and the water capacity of the side tanks was as much as 2,700 gallons. The front and rear bogies, instead of being the then usual 'swing link' type, had sliding centre pieces moving in supports attached to transverse members across the frame and controlled by horizontal coiled springs – an innovation which worked well in practice, though it was rather costly to maintain.

Initial testing of No. 327 suggested that it could easily do all that was expected of it, so the 4 – 6 – 0 then still under construction was modified to be of the same 4 – 6 – 4 type, the already-cut-out frames being extended to the rear; the tender originally set aside for it, which was complete, was put into store and eventually used on a new 2 – 6 – 0 mixed traffic engine. However, No. 327 now began to show a serious fault, that of instability. Running at a speed with a test train at Hassocks, on the main line, all its coupled wheels left the track, though the front and rear bogie wheel stayed on it. This was the first of a number of derailments which culminated in one at Fishbourne, which also happened when the

No. 328, in LB&SCR livery, after installation of well tanks. The headcode indicates a special train between London Bridge and Brighton, or *vice versa*. Taken in December 1918.
LCGB Ken Nunn Collection

No. 328, not in very clean condition, resting between duties. Taken in 1920.
Locomotive Publishing Co.

No. B 328, in SR livery, taken
at Brighton, September 1931.
Photomatic

engine was travelling at speed, in November 1914. By
this time No. 327's fellow-Baltic had been completed at
Brighton, so both it and No. 327 were stored for six
months while modifications were worked out to make
them more stable.

It seemed necessary to get the weight of water that
the engines carried into a different position where its
movement from side to side did not cause rolling. A
somewhat drastic solution was determined upon; a large
well-tank was built between the frames of each engine,
where there were fortunately no moving parts such as
cranks, rods or eccentrics, as would have been the case
had Stephenson's valve gear been used. The well was
made large enough to hold most of the water, and the
side tanks, though still remaining as a prominent external feature, were blocked off at the level of 15 inches
above their floors. To compensate for the extra weight
of the well tank thinner steel was used for the upper
parts of the side tank casings and lighter supporting
brackets were placed beneath them; baffle plates were
placed within all the water-containing sections to prevent the surging of water when they were no longer full.
Side tanks and well tank were connected by channels
in such a way that the former emptied first, so that on
a 50-mile journey they would contain water only for the
first few miles.

One drawback of the new arrangement was that the
feed-water heating system that had been installed inside
the tanks had to be removed, so that the injectors now
filled the boiler with cold water. Billinton therefore experimented with two other methods of heating the feed-
water in turn, one of which required the removal of
superheater elements from their flues, which of course
lessened the amount of superheat; the feed water was
then passed through tubes within the flues. Experimen-
ting went on until 1923. Some saving in coal consumption resulted, but at the same time maintenance became
more expensive, so the system was eventually discard-
ed; it was in any case only used in the prototype, No. 327.

At the end of 1918, once the War had ended, Billinton ordered five more similar 4 – 6 – 4s to be built.

There was an initial delay, construction being held up
through disorganisation at the Works due to the War,
and they took their places in the queue with other new
engines in October 1919 No. 329 was completed and
named *Stephenson*; Nos. 330 and 331, un-named, following two months later; No. 332 came out in March 1922,
and No. 333 named *Remembrance* as a war Memorial
locomotive completed the sequence in April. All were
stationed at Brighton and showed their capability by
running the fastest trains to time in all weathers. One
of them, No, 329 suffered an undignified accident at
the end of September, when an error of judgement on
the part of its driver caused it to over-run the turntable
at Brighton, push its way through a brick wall and end
up in the roadway on the other side.

After the grouping of 1923 the Baltics lost their umber
livery one by one as they were shopped, beginning with
No. 333 in May 1924 and ending up with No. 332 in
November 1925; they then received the standard SR
green livery with the name SOUTHERN on each tank
and the number beneath in yellow letters and figures.
No. 329, *Stephenson*, and No. 333, *Remembrance*, kept their
names but the prototype, No. 327 had its name removed.

Various small alterations were made to some
members of the class over the subsequent years; such
as modifications to the blast-pipe orifices, which slightly lessened coal consumption, the removal of the
cylinder tail rods and the replacement of the Robinson-
type superheaters by those of Maunsell's design. In
1932 – 1933 they were re-numbered by having the figure
2 put in front of their original numbers in place of the
B prefix.

At first they resigned supreme on the Brighton fast
trains, but from 1925 onwards other locomotives began
to replace them. Maunsell's first batch of 2 – 6 – 4 'River'
tanks commenced working alongside them soon after
their delivery, and while not very popular with the Central Section crews, who found them unsteady at speed,
proved that they could, with their higher boiler pressure
and more up-to-date front end design, match the performance of the Baltics despite being several tons

Above: No. 329 named *Stephenson* on the tank side (name and number only just visible) working a train out of Victoria. The head-code indicates a London Bridge – Crystal Palace train, and is misleading!

F. Moore's Railway Photographs

National Railway Museum

Below: No. 322 newly painted in SR colours.

SOUTHERN
B
332

Above: No. 2328 (after the omission of the 'B' prefix and the addition of 2,000 to the number) heading a down Pullman Car express to Eastbourne near Lewes in 1935.
Photomatic

Below: No. B 333 in SR colours on up Pullman Car express, passing Honor Oak Park station, June 1931.*Photomatic*

lighter. In 1926 the 'Rivers' were taken off the principal fast trains, most of them being transferred to the Eastern Section, and were replaced by a batch of Glasgow-built 'King Arthur' 4–6–0s specially fitted with 6-wheel tenders, and these latter pushed the 4–6–4s more and more on to secondary duties, though the prestige business train, the 60-minute 'City Limited' from Brighton to London Bridge and back, remained their preserve.

However, the entire disappearance of steam from the express routes of the Central Section was approaching, for the SR board was set on their electrification. Gradually the third rail began to extend further and further to the South, so that even the days of the 'King Arthurs' there were numbered. In these circumstances, what was to be done with the Baltics? Their quality had been proved, but there was no room for their use as tank engines on express duties on the Western and Eastern sections, where the end-to-end running distances were much greater than the 51 miles between London and Brighton. It was decided to reconstruct them as tender engines – the same fate as had already befallen the 'Rivers' after the fatal accident at Sevenoaks in August 1927; the Baltics, however, suffered no downgrading from express passenger status, as happened to the 2–6–4s, which lost not only their tanks but their names; on the contrary they were *all* now named, as *Stephenson* had been, each after a famous engineer, except for *Remembrance*, which kept its War Memorial status and dedicatory plaque, and they took their places as associates of the 'King Arthurs' and 'Lord Nelsons' on the Western Section. Rebuilding took place at Eastleigh Works between April 1935 and April 1936. All were eventually taken over in 1948 when the railways were nationalised, and were given the lined black secondary passenger livery, some in the meantime having in their last years as SR engines attained the splendour of Bulleid's malachite green. Final withdrawal occurred between August 1955 and July 1957, by which time they had all been as long or longer in their rebuilt state as in their original condition. All that now remains of them is a set of name-plates and memorial plaques from *Remembrance*, preserved for a while at Brighton Works but now in the care of the National Railway Museum, York.

One is fortunate in having a good deal of information as to the performance of these locomotives before they were reconstructed, though it is almost entirely limited to the main line between London and Brighton. The route was a popular one with the train-timing stopwatch fraternity, and the writer confesses to having travelled on it to record the running of the early electric express trains, including the *Brighton Belle*, during the mid-thirties, using day return tickets; no doubt others before him did the same, for it only cost a few shillings, and for an extra one-and-sixpence one could come back on the afternoon or evening Pullman. It seems best to set out a number of logs of runs in each direction, made in chronological order, and comment on each one.

The main line between Victoria and Brighton was not by any means an easy route, as the gradient profile shows. Within a total of 51 miles three separate well-marked summits have to be surmounted; the ruling gra-

dient is 1 in 264, though a few slightly steeper pitches are found between Coulsdon and Quarry Box and for short stretches on the London side of Croydon. No other main line out of London can show as many 'collar-work' requirements in so short a distance. Between Croydon and both Victoria and London Bridge there were quite a few service slacks; onwards to Brighton, however, there were none in either direction, which meant that there could be fast travelling in the dips at Horley and near Wivelsfield; however, the down grades were too short to allow very high speeds to be attained. The Baltics, with their large cylinders, were designed to climb banks vigorously and recover quickly from out-of-course slacks and signal delays; they were not expected to make up time by very fast downhill running. Timekeeping was rather easier in the southbound direction, since delays were more common North of Croydon than South of it, and it was easier to recoup the lost minutes on the way to Brighton than in the return direction.

In the down direction the first run tabulated, made soon after the grouping and with a substantial load, was badly checked before Croydon. No. 328 then made a vigorous effort as far as Quarry Box, but after that took things too easily to recover time, the 70 m.p.h. rate being nowhere reached; a final check before Preston Park

DOWN JOURNEYS:

Locomotive:	328		330		333		332
Gross load in tons:	380		320*		310		385
Miles	m. s.	spd.	m. s.	spd.	m. s.	spd.	m. s.
0.0 Victoria	00 00				00 00		
	PWS						
2.7 Clapham Jn.	06 30				05 35	47	
4.7 Balham					08 05	44½	
	PWS					58	
7.5 Norbury					11 24		
0.0 London Br.			00 00				00 00
2.8 New Cr. Gt.			05 05	54½			05 20
5.5 Forest Hill			08 50	36½			09 40
8.6 Norwood Jn							14 05
10.5 E. Croydon	18 40		14 55		14 41		16 10
13.5 Purley					18 00		19 50
15.0 Coulsdon N.	24 15		20 35		19 39	55	21 30
17.5 M.P. 17¼		45	25 45	41½	22 28	50	24 50
21.9 Earlswood	32 10		28 40	69	26 45		29 15
26.0 Horley	36 00	67	32 10	77½	30 11	77	32 40
29.5 3 Bridges	39 45		35 20	65	33 16		35 45
				sigs.			
32.0 M.P. 31¾	42 45	44	38 05		35 43	60	38 17
34.1 Balcombe					37 42		40 20
				71½	sigs.		
38.0 Haywds H.	49 00	66	44 10		42 07		43 40
41.1 Keymer Jn.	51 55		47 10		45 05	68	46 20
				sigs.			
50.0 Lewes			60 40				
46.2 M.P. 46		51			sigs.		51 25
	PWS						
49.6 Preston P.	60 55				55 54		54 40
					sigs.		
50.9 Brighton	64 10				58 41		57 48

All distances from London Bridge are 0.2 mile less from East Croydon than shown from Victoria.

* Two coaches slipped at Horley, reducing the load by 70 tons.

caused the arrival to be just over four minutes late; net time was 60 minutes, as scheduled. The second run, on an evening business train from London Bridge to Eastbourne, was with a lighter load, from which two coaches were slipped at Horley. The start was brisk; things were then taken a little more easily as far as the summit near Merstham; a spurt then followed, and with a much lightened load a high minimum speed might have been expected at Balcombe tunnel entrance; instead a signal check hampered progress. Speed had risen again to 71 ½ at Wivelsfield before the slowing for the curve at Keymer Junction, and another signal check was experienced at the approach to Lewes, but an early arrival there was none the less achieved, with a net time from London bridge of 58 minutes.

The third and fourth runs in the table were made on an historic occasion, on the last day of December 1932 when the steam-hauled 'Southern Belle' made its final journey to Brighton, after which the all-electric 'Brighton Belle' took its place. Fittingly the memorial engine No. 333, *Remembrance*, was selected to haul it. It gave an extremely fine performance, gaining time steadily so that it was about 4 minutes ahead of schedule at Balcombe; then a signal check gave notice that the road ahead was not clear enough for a continuation of the previous

effort. Further checks followed on the approach to Brighton, which was nevertheless reached 1 ¼ minutes early. Net time was only 54 ½ minutes. The fourth run was on the last steam-hauled 'City Limited' from London Bridge; with a much heavier load but no checks of any kind, over two minutes were gained on schedule. The recorder noted no speeds, but passing time suggests a similar top speed to that of the last-quoted run at Horley, and a high minimum at Balcombe tunnel, with a maximum in the seventies somewhere near Wivelsfield.

In the opposite direction No. 332, when only a few months old, took the 'City Limited' up from Brighton at a time when the schedule was 62 minutes. In general it was an undistinguished performance, though 74 m.p.h. was reached at Horley; after Purley signal checks, including a dead stand outside London Bridge station for over 3 ½ minutes, made the train 3 ¼ minutes late into the terminus. No. 327, on the 12.20 p.m. from Brighton, with a considerably heavier train, displayed more energy, topping the summit at Clayton tunnel entrance at 48 and continuing the same effort until Balcombe; speed was then eased to Horley but a vigorous climb followed to Quarry Box. Croydon was passed a minute early, and things were then taken

UP JOURNEYS:

Locomotive:	332		327		330		331	
Gross load in tons:	380		385*		310		430	
Miles	m. s.	speed	m. s.	speed	m. s.	speed	m. s.	sp.
0.0 Brighton	00 00		00 00		00 00		00 00	
1.3 Preston Park	04 05				03 06		03 25	
4.8 M.P. 46	09 10	40 ½	08 30	48	07 25	53	08 10	46
7.1 Hassocks	11 55		11 00	64	09 54		10 40	
9.8 Keymer Jn.			13 30			58		
12.9 Hayward's Heath	17 40	61	16 20	71 ½	14 58		15 55	
16.6 Balcombe	22 00	54			18 46	60	20 10	
					PWS			
19.0 M.P.	31 ¾		21 45	55 ½	21 24		22 45	50
21.4 Three Bridges	26 40		25 05		24 15		25 05	
24.9 Horley	29 50	74	28 20	68	27 12	75	28 25	65
29.0 Earlswood	34 15		32 20		30 56		32 30	
32.1 Quarry Box	38 25	44 ½	35 40	50 ½	34 05	55	35 55	48
							PWS	
35.9 Coulsdon North			39 45				41.20	
37.4 Purley	44 10	65		68	39 14	72 ½		
	sigs.							
40.4 East Croydon	49 00		44 00		41 53		46 45	
43.4 Norbury					45 01			
			PWS					
46.2 Balham					47 57			
48.2 Clapham Jn.			54 25		50 02		55 55	
					sigs.		sigs.	
50.9 Victoria			59 25		56 55		62 40	
42.1 Norwood Jn.	50 55							
45.2 Forest Hill	53 45	63 ½						
47.9 New Cross Gate	57 05							
	sig.	stop						
50.7 London Bridge	65 15							

Former 4–6–4 No. 2333 now newly rebuilt at Eastleigh as 4–6–0, retaining name and commemorative plaque.
Photomatic

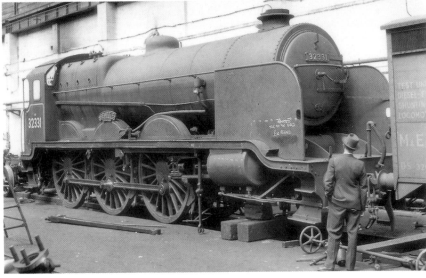

In BR days. No. 32331 *Beattie*, after being rebuilt as a 4–6–0, is undergoing repair at Eastleigh. *Photomatic*

easily to Victoria, which was reached half a minute before time despite a permanent way slack at Balham.

With a somewhat lighter train No. 330 made an excellent run, of which the hill-climbing was the most notable feature, the minimum of 60 up Balcombe bank being very good indeed, as was the unusual speed of 72½ at Purley before the slowing of Croydon. Despite a permanent slack after Balcombe and adverse signals between Clapham Junction and Victoria more than three minutes were gained on the 60-minute schedule; the net time was about 55½ minutes. Finally, with the unusually heavy load of 430 tons No. 331 made a very good run, climbing the banks vigorously and being well on time at Quarry Box, but a permanent way delay and signals on before Victoria caused the train to be 2¾ minutes late into the terminus.

These performances show the Brighton Baltics to have been very successful locomotives. They had been tailored to perform a particular task on the LBSCR main line, and once they had been modified to get rid of the large tank locomotive's besetting sin, rolling at speed to a dangerous extent, they proved equal to the requirements of Central Section main line express work, even with loads of 400 tons and more. They could no doubt have given many more years of service on the principal fast trains, had the work remained there for them to do. But electrification made them redundant in their existing state, and although their lives were honourably extended by rebuilding them as express passenger 4–6–0s the sparkle had gone out after reconstruction; they could not match either the 'Arthurs' or 'Nelsons' when asked to perform alongside them on the Western Section, and were eventually relegated to secondary passenger duties. They, more than most locomotives, were horses built for courses, and when the courses were taken away they had lost their *raison d'être*; rebuilt, they still looked good, but so far as performance was concerned it was

. . . . . *the glimmer of twilight; Never glad, confident morning again.*

4. CROSTHWAIT'S BALTICS FOR THE BELFAST—BANGOR LINE

The third design in Great Britain for a 4 – 6 – 4 tank locomotive arose in what might be considered an unlikely place – the workshops of a minor Irish railway. The Belfast & County Down Company was exactly what its name indicated; it served the latter area fairly comprehensively but did not stray outside it. Its main route was only just over 40 miles long; it also put out a number of branches to reach the chief centres of population, the last of which was completed in 1906. However, this had scarcely happened when the first signs appeared of the enemy which was to compete with it and eventually bring about the disappearance of most of it – the petrol motor vehicle. By the end of the 'twenties road competition was already being keenly felt, and after the Second World War the system was taken over by the Ulster Transport Authority, which closed one section of it after another, eventually leaving open only the 12 ½ miles from Belfast to Bangor.

The latter section had always been the busiest part of the system. Bangor itself and many places between it and the Ulster capital became dormitories for city workers, the former resort in this respect resembling Southend-on-Sea at the end of the LTSR. As on the latter line, the BCDR passenger trains were operated by tank locomotives which from the beginning of the century were mostly 4 – 4 – 2s with inside cylinders. These could cope perfectly well with the fairly light and leisurely-scheduled trains from Belfast to Downpatrick and Newcastle, but the residential services along the south side of Belfast Lough had to be more sharply-timed to give business men in the capital an acceptably quick run from home to work and back, and these appeared by the end of the First World War to need engines of greater power.

J.L. Crosthwait, who came from being District Locomotive Superintendent at Waterford on the Great Southern & Western Railway to succeed R.G. Miller as Locomotive Superintendent on the BCDR in 1919, found on his arrival that the existing 4 – 4 – 2 tank types were being hard-pressed on the Bangor service. The most important trains on this section were the morning up and evening down business expresses, made up of six-wheeled stock which was daily packed with passengers who expected good timekeeping in return for the prices of their season tickets. A six-coupled design seemed called for; exactly why the Baltic type was fixed upon is not known. A rumour became current later that the Locomotive Department had been under pressure from one of the Company's directors who had been impressed by the size and appearance of Billinton's 4 – 6 – 4 prototype on the LBSCR and wanted to see something similar on the Bangor line and that while

R.G. Miller had scouted the idea during his superintendency, Crosthwait, being newly-appointed and still finding his feet, agreed to the suggestion. At any rate a specification for such an engine was drawn up and Beyer Peacock & Company of Manchester was given the order to construct four.

There has been some question as to who was responsible for the design – whether it was entirely the product of the drawing office of the BCDR or whether the engine as a whole originated at Beyer Peacock's. Probably neither suggestion is wholly true as it stands. A new type of locomotive, very different from its BCDR predecessors, would have needed to have many details worked out by experienced draughtsmen who were familiar with the planning of such large machines, and this may well have been done in Manchester, but one need not doubt that they worked to a specification for which Crosthwait was responsible. The new locomotives were delivered at Belfast at the beginning of 1920 and numbered from 24 to 27.

They were smaller and lighter than any of the other 4 – 6 – 4 locomotives dealt with in this book, but nevertheless the largest and heaviest ever to run in Ireland up to that time. The 5 ft. diameter boiler had its dome on the first ring, was attached to a Belpaire firebox with a sizeable grate, and in common with all BCDR engines had no superheating equipment; saturated steam from the regulator in the dome went straight to the steam chest and thence to the two outside cylinders by way of piston valves placed above them, the latter being operated by Walschaert's valve gear. Inspection of the detailed drawings of the valve and cylinder arrangements have suggested that a 'negative lead' was given when steam was admitted to the cylinders; if the inference is correct, this was unusual. (The word 'lead' in a locomotive context is applied to the arrangement by which steam is admitted to the cylinder slightly ahead of the moment when the piston comes to the end of its stroke, so that a 'cushion' of it is inserted between the moving piston and the end wall of the cylinder. This makes for smoother running; however, if in these four engines there *was* a negative lead, steam was not admitted until *after* the end of the stroke. This would improve the draught and steaming of the engine but at the expense of fuel. Possibly the adjustment was deliberate).

The coupled wheels were on the small side, which was desirable if the locomotive were to have the ability to accelerate rapidly but did not need to attain high speeds, and the coupled wheel-base was only 12 ft 2 ins long, so that the total adhesion weight was concentrated on a very short length of track; for this reason it could not regularly be used on the more lightly-laid parts of the

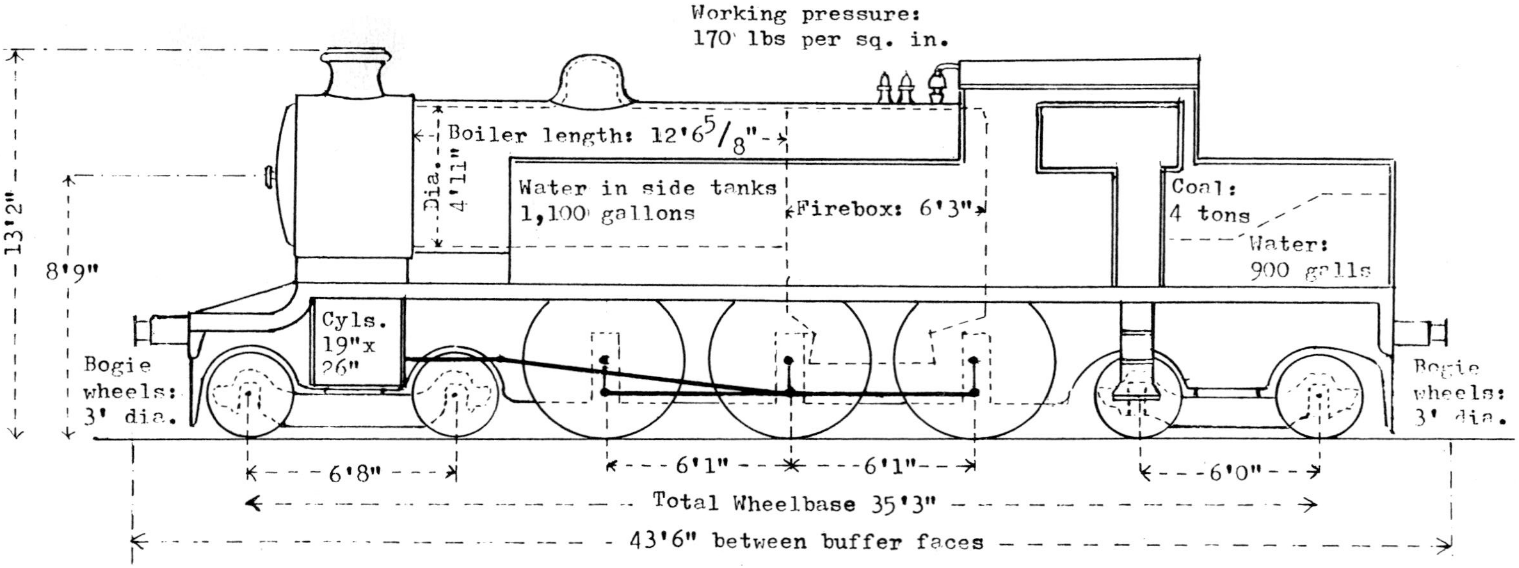
Working pressure:
170 lbs per sq. in.
Boiler length: 12'6 5/8"
Dia. 4'11"
Water in side tanks
1,100 gallons
Firebox: 6'3"
Coal:
4 tons
Water:
900 galls
Cyls.
19"x
26"
13'2"
8'9"
Bogie
wheels:
3' dia.
Bogie
wheels:
3' dia.
6'8"
6'1"
6'1"
6'0"
Total Wheelbase 35'3"
43'6" between buffer faces

CROSTHWAIT'S SUCCESSFUL DESIGN OF BALTIC TANK FOR THE BELFAST & COUNTY DOWN RAILWAY

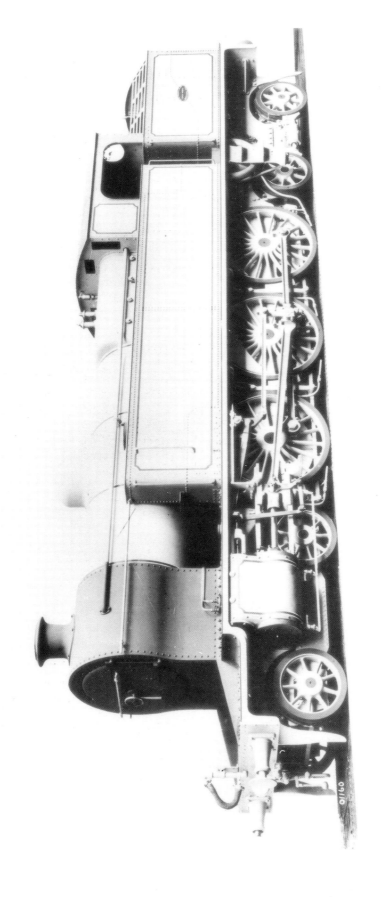

Works photograph of one of the B&CDR 4–6–4s taken at Beyer Peacock's works before receiving B&CDR livery.
Greater Manchester Museum of Science & Industry

4 – 6 – 4 tank engine No. 22 newly-painted in the Company's livery.

Railway Photographs, Liverpool

Company's system, but only on the line to Bangor. The coupled wheels and bogie wheels all had laminated springs, those for the former also having equalising levers for the better distribution of shocks from the track. Three sandboxes on either side supplied their contents to the coupled wheels, the leading pair being fed in from in front, the rear pair from behind and the central pair from either side. Steam-operated brakes worked on the coupled and rear bogie wheels.

The cab was sizeable but had no side windows. The bunker had space for 4 tons of coal, beneath which was a tank holding 900 gallons of water; each side tank also held 550 gallons when full. The engine's total weight in working order was less than 82 tons, the absence of superheating equipment partly explaining this.

While these locomotives certainly had the ability to tackle the Belfast-Bangor trains more forcefully than their 4 – 4 – 2 predecessors, they were not popular with their crews, and particularly not with the firemen because they had enormous appetite for coal, which during the period of the Second World War, when they had some hard slogging to do, could rise to over 80 lb per mile. When in full cry climbing a bank their exhausts could be heard far and wide. They undoubtedly steamed well; on the other hand, what the Board of Directors had to say when the fuel consumption was brought to its notice can only be surmised, and if it be true that their acquisition was the result of one director's pressure on the Locomotive Department one wonders what might have been said to *him*. The surprising thing is that these engines lasted as long as they did – right up to the end of the Company's existence and beyond. One of them

was not disposed of until the end of June 1956, by which time it was 36½ years old.

The only scheduled services on which the 4 – 6 – 4s were used were those on the Bangor line, but there was one occasion soon after their delivery when one of them was tried out on the main line with a long train of livestock vehicles, to see how it responded to a heavy load. According to E.M. Patterson, who wrote a history of the railway,

.... the occasion was Fair Day at Ballynahinch. The Baltic brought out 35 loaded trucks from the branch terminus, and a further 15 were added at the Junction. Thereafter the journey to Belfast was not a happy one. The sluggish Baltic failed to keep the couplings tight, and in one of the hollows past Saintfield the train broke in two places. The performance was repeated near Ballygown and the train was brought into Comber piecemeal. The experiment was not repeated.

It comes as something of a surprise to discover that records of the running of these engines have been made. One is indebted to Mr. R.M. Arnold, who in his entertaining book *Steam over Belfast Lough* includes logs of journeys behind different types of locomotive during the years immediately after the Second World War. I have extracted four of these, made behind Baltics. The gradient profile of this line shows that the first 4½ miles as far as Holywood are level (though having curves which deter fast running) but then follow 2½ miles of steep gradients varying between 1 in 73 and 1 in 114 to the summit at mile post 7 beyond Craigavad. After that, there is a falling tendency, also steeply-graded, with an intervening minor summit between Craigavad and Helen's Bay.

On the first run in the table, with a non-stop train between Belfast (Queen's Quay) and Bangor West, No. 23, with a load of 260 tons, attained 50 m.p.h. at Holywood, fell to 26 at Craigavad and reached 50 again at Carnalea before steam was shut off for the stop at Bangor West. With the same load on the same train No. 24 made a slower start but a better climb to Craigavad, and with a very smart finish just beat No. 23's time. In the opposite direction, from Bangor, with a load of 270 tons and a stop at Helen's Bay, the highest speed attained was 55 m.p.h. at Marino near the foot of the descent to Holywood. One notes from the table of logs Mr Arnold provides that the Northern Counties Committee's 2 – 6 – 4 tanks could do far better than the Baltics; with a similar load one of them reached 64 at the same point and 67 beyond Holywood, and with a slightly lighter train another one reached a maximum of 70 miles an hour at the foot of this bank. The Baltics showed up best on the stopping trains, such as the one logged in the last column; it will be noted that two of the start-to-stop timings were less than the start-to-pass times in the previous log, over very short distance, though admittedly with a lighter load.

As already mentioned, these engines, in spite of the fact that they were in some respects so unsatisfactory, lasted a long time, and only met their doom when the BCDR itself came to an end and its stock and property were sold under the auctioneer's hammer in 1956.

LOGS OF JOURNEYS BEHIND B&CDR BALTIC TANKS:

Locomotive:	23	24
Load in tons:	260	260

Miles		m. s.	m. s.
0.0	Belfast (Queen's Quay)	00 00	00 00
1.8	Sydenham	03 58	04 20
4.5	Holywood	07 25	07 41
5.4	Marino	08 46	09 00
6.1	Cultra	09 55	10 05
6.7	Craigavad	11 15	11 20
9.0	Helen's Bay	15 11	15 11
10.5	Carnalea	17 04	17 05
11.2	Bangor West	18 27	18 18

Locomotive:	25	22
Load in tons:	270	150

Miles		m. s.	m. s.
0.0	Bangor	00 00	00 00
1.1	Bangor West	04 14	03 54
1.8	Carnalea	05 43	02 18
3.3	Helen's Bay	08 16	03 47
5.6	Craigavad	06 02	05 20
6.2	Cultra		01 21
6.9	Marino	07 32	02 38
7.8	Holywood	08 43	02 12
10.5	Sydenham	12 02	05 02
			sigs.
12.3	Belfast (Queens's Quay)	15 05	04 16

4 – 6 – 4 No. 25 heading a Belfast – Bangor train of 4 and 6-wheeled coaches.   *LCGB Ken Nunn Collection*

5. RUTHERFORD'S BALTICS FOR THE FURNESS LINE:

The Furness Railway, centered on Barrow-in-Furness, the largest town in what is now Cumbria and an important industrial centre with shipbuilding as a main occupation, was one of the larger independent railway systems of Great Britain outside the eleven main companies in England and Wales and the five in Scotland; it had a monopoly of rail transport along the northern shore of Morecambe Bay and the North Lancashire and Cumberland coastline as far as Whitehaven. Its main line extended from Carnforth, where it made a junction with the LNWR, to Whitehaven, following a sinuous route which mostly hugged the coast and here and there bridged wide estuaries, though Grange-over-Sands, Ulverston, Barrow, Millom, Ravenglass and Seascale. It put out three branches, one from Arnside which linked up with the LNWR again at Hincaster Junction north of Milnthorpe, one from Ulverston which reached the southern end of Windermere at Lakeside, and one from Foxfield near the crossing of the Duddon estuary which led to Coniston Water and Coniston village. The first afforded a short cut from Barrow to Kendal and was

used by mineral trains from the Furness area to the North Eastern Railway's branch from Teeside across Stainmore to Tebay. The second and third were largely for the benefit of tourists who could approach the Lake District from the south by their means. The Furness Railway had a distinct individuality, expressed in its colourful livery of Indian red for locomotives and white upper and blue lower panels for passenger coaches. But it could not be regarded as a fast line; the route it followed was not adapted for high speed traffic. Journeys were taken at a leisurely pace, and though some of the trains included corridor coaches there were no restaurant or buffet cars.

At the end of the First World War the need was felt for a few really powerful locomotives. Since 1890 recourse had principally been had to 4 – 4 – 0s for passenger services; these had been built in small batches since that date. Freight duties were chiefly undertaken by 0-6-0 tender engines. There was also a handful of tank locomotives, mostly of the 0-6-0 arrangement, though a few were 4 – 4 – 2s. In addition there were two steam

No. 11101 (formerly FR No. 116) posing for an official photograph before receiving LMSR livery. Note the massive framing and front wheel guards projecting from buffer beam.
National Railway Museum

No. 11101 in LMSR black livery, about to haul a train of former FR stock. Probably taken at Barrow-in-Furness.
National Railway Museum

rail-motors for the Lakeside and Coniston branches. During the War the locomotive department pondered on what sort of larger engine should be designed. The Locomotive Superintendent, W Pettigrew, does not seem to have given this problem much active consideration - he was due to retire in March 1918 in any case - but it was very much in the mind of the Chief Draughtsman, E Sharples. Why this particular type of wheel arrangement should have been chosen is uncertain, but the LBSCR had shown that a Baltic tank could be successfully used on all *its* services, whose longest through runs approximated in distance to that of the Furness Railway from Carnforth to Whitehaven, and the fast running near Hassocks and Fishbourne which had been the occasions of Brighton 4 – 6 – 4s becoming derailed was not really a possibility along the Cumbrian coast. Possibly the difficulty of fitting a 4 – 6 – 0 with a tender on to existing turntables may also have weighed with the FR locomotive department.

In November 1918, as soon as the War had come to an end, D.L. Rutherford, who had been the FR's Chief Engineer before Pettigrew's retirement and who now assumed the latter's duties as well as retaining his own, recommended the purchase of five 4 – 6 – 4 tank engines and after the Board had agreed to this tenders were invited from locomotive building firms. To each of these a specification with a drawing was sent, but contractors were also told they were free to suggest another design if it fitted in with the general dimensions on the drawing and specification. The North British Locomotive Company took advantage of this and suggested a modified version of the 4 – 6 – 2 tank engine which they recently constructed for the Caledonian Railway to a design by W Pickersgill. However, this proposal had to be rejected since the CR engine, having outside cylinders, was too wide for the FR's rather tight loading gauge. Eventually Kitson & Co of Leeds offered to construct the engines as designed; its tender was accepted in February 1919 on the understanding that all five locomotives were to be delivered by June 1920. In fact

they were not ready till the end of that year, four being supplied in November and the fifth two months later.

At the suggestion of the builders some alteration were made in the original design. The firebox was lengthened and given two square feet extra grate area. In regard to the boiler, a two-ring one had been specified, but what actually happened was that Kitsons, who had built a number of 2 – 8 – 0s to the design of J.G. Robinson, Locomotive Superintendent on the Great Central Railway, for the Ministry of Munitions during the war, found it more convenient to substitute a three-ring boiler such as the latter engines had been given, since it was only a few inches longer and of the same diameter. The bogie wheelbases were also slightly increased, and the capacity of the tanks, which included a well-tank beneath the coal bunkers, was also slightly raised. For some unknown reason the piston valves were reduced in diameter from 10 to 8 inches.

As with all other locomotives built for the FR inside cylinders were used; this was the only British Baltic type to have no outside cylinders. A somewhat surprising omission was any sort of superheater. The FR had experimented at an earlier date with the 'Phoenix' type of smokebox superheater, but had not found it successful, and it seems to have been decided that the fitting of fire-tube superheaters would not cause a sufficient reduction in fuel costs and other expenses to outweigh the cost of installation. For the first time on this line the Belpaire firebox made its appearance. Particular care was taken with the springing of the coupled wheels, since the permanent way on the FR was not of the highest standard, and subsidences in the track were not uncommon where the line ran over the sites of old mine workings. The leading and trailing coupled wheels had laminated springs, the central pair helical springs. Wheel-sanding was done with wet sand, which would adhere more readily to the rails and be less likely to be blown away by strong side winds after being dropped, such winds being frequent in many exposed places along the line, such as the viaducts across the

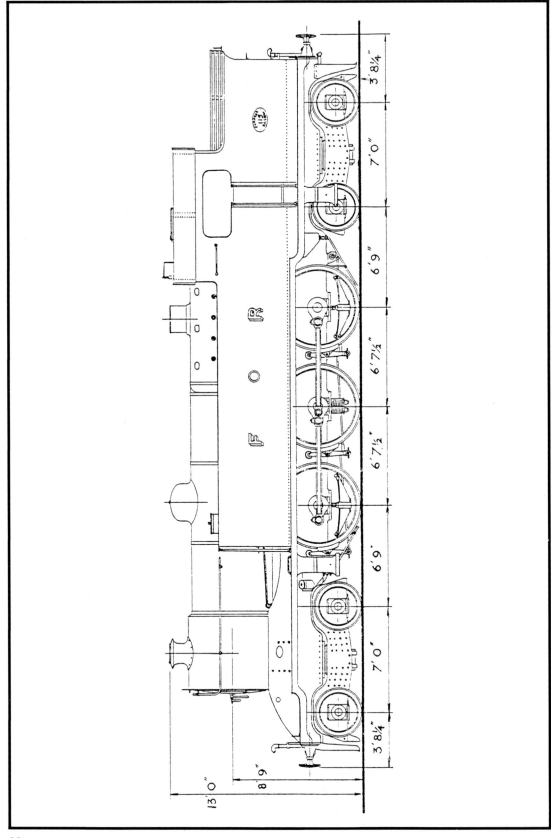

RUTHERFORD 2 CYLINDER 4–6–4T BUILT BY KITSON OF LEEDS IN 1920 FOR THE FURNESS RAILWAY

estuaries of the Kent and Leven.

The bunker capacity was, for a tank locomotive, quite large. The water-provision was adequate on a line where no long non-stop runs were scheduled; all trains passing through Barrow in any case stopped there for at least five minutes, which gave time to top up the water supply. The engines were built to the limits of the FR loading gauge - so much that when one of them had to remain overnight at Whitehaven it could not be accommodated in the engine shed but had to remain in the open. In their completed form, numbered 115 to 119, they looked massive and, painted in the FR Indian red livery, with FR in gilded letters on each side tank and the Company's coat of arms between, they were a splendid sight. Particularly noticeable was the prominent upward projection of the framing beneath the smokebox.

All five locomotives were based at Barrow during the short period of FR ownership, and after that railway had been taken over by the LMSR this still remained generally the case. After a period when they were confined to freight services they were transferred to work the main passenger trains on the FR main line, which were timed in about 2½ hours between Carnforth and Whitehaven, with several intermediate stops. However, one or two of them strayed on to LMSR metals. For about a year during 1925 – 1926 one of them headed a through train from Barrow to Manchester and back, and at about the same time another found its way back on to the Manchester – Buxton line, where it joined one of the ex-LTSR Baltics and two of Hughes' 4-cylinder Baltics (to be described later) on that steeply-graded route. After passing under LMSR ownership they first received the crimson lake passenger locomotive livery and were re-numbered 11100 – 11104 on the side tanks. Later they received the less prestigious black livery, with the letters LMS on the side tanks and the numbers on the bunkers.

The Furness Baltics proved popular with their crews and were well able to cope with the chief trains, tackling the heavy gradients between Ulverston and Barrow with ease. No records of their day-to-day running appear to exist, which is hardly surprising as train-timers would scarcely have felt it worth while making logs of performances on leisurely schedules. One would not imagine that speeds in excess of 60 m.p.h. were called for, even on the fastest bookings such as the 27-minute schedule between Carnforth and Ulverston, 18¾ miles. With the usual loadings these locomotives provided a great reserve of power and were appreciated for that reason. In the words of O.S. Nock,

.... their introduction revolutionised Furness hill-climbing, especially on the semi-fast trains on which they were largely put to work, of which the morning service to London is an example.

This latter train in 1922 was the Company's fastest; it left Whitehaven at 11.35 a.m., called only at St. Bees, Seascale, Revenglass and Millom to Barrow, reached at 12.55 p.m.; after a 5-minute stop there and a subsequent halt at Ulverston, Carnforth was reached at 1.55, the through carriage arriving at Euston at 7.20 p.m. In the opposite direction the 3.43 p.m. which included through coaches from London that left Euston at 10.30 a.m., took 7 minutes longer, but made two extra stops and waited at Barrow for eight minutes, so it was comparable with the up train. Over the 9¾ miles from Barrow to Ulverston, which included a 4½-mile bank that had many stretches at 1 in 100 or steeper, the former train was scheduled in 18 minutes start to re-start and here the revolutionary hill-climbing was no doubt in evidence.

The Furness Baltics did not have a very long life, the first being withdrawn in 1934 after less than 15 years' service. Three others were withdrawn the following year, but for some reason No. 11103 survived for another five years and was not sent to be scrapped until December 1940.

No. 11102 taking water at Barrow into the right-hand tank; note the water pipe going over the top of engine boiler.

C.J. Fryer Collection

6. WHITELEGG'S BALTICS FOR THE GLASGOW & SOUTH WESTERN RAILWAY

It was perhaps only to be expected that after Robert Whitelegg (following an interval when he first went into agricultural engineering and then, during the First World War, acted as a Government advisor in railway matters) was appointed in August 1918 as Locomotive Superintendent on the Glasgow & South Western Railway, he would respond to a situation similar to the one that had faced him on the LTSR in a similar way. The GSWR was of course a much larger concern than the railway in Essex had been, with a main trunk route over which through trains ran from Glasgow to Carlisle *en route* for London and other English cities, and with an important secondary route to Stranraer that connected there with the short sea route to Belfast. However, it also had a considerable outer suburban traffic between Glasgow and the Clyde coast, carrying many commuters who lived at or near such places as Greenock, Largs and Ayr. The distances from Fenchurch Street to Tilbury and Southend-on-Sea are comparable to those between St. Enoch station in Glasgow and the above-mentioned towns. Moreover, just as the LTSR faced competition for its South end traffic from the GER, which had its own route there from Liverpool Street, so also the GWSR had a rival which also served Greenock, the Caledonian Railway. These shorter lines were important and, like the LTSR had been growing busier, so that train loads had been increasing.

For these services a more powerful type of engine was needed which could accelerate rapidly from stops. In regard to its motive power, the GSWR had fallen back somewhat. It had 17 two-cylinder 4 – 6 – 0s, only two of which had been superheated, which were needed for the through trains on the Dumfries and Carlisle line. For the trains on the coast lines reliance was placed mostly on 4 – 4 – 0s, mostly of Manson's design or rebuilt by him, as well as a few constructed by Peter Drummond, some of which had been given superheaters. There were no passenger tank engines suitable for fast running, and few tank engines of any kind. Yet the coast services seemed to call aloud for such locomotives as long as they were of adequate power. This must have been very plain to Whitelegg when he took office in 1918 after Drummond's death. However, his first priority was get the existing locomotive stock, run down by war work and lack of adequate maintenance, back into better shape. In the course of doing so rebuilt most of the Manson 4 – 6 – 0s, and did the same with Manson's solitary four-cylinder 4 – 4 – 0, which was named *Lord Glenarthur*, turning it into the most massive-looking engine of that wheel

arrangement ever to have appeared on any British railway up to that time.

Eventually the opportunity came to build some new locomotives. Money for them was at first lacking, but by the middle of 1920 he had over £25,000 standing to his credit in the 'Arrears for Locomotive Renewals' account. The Ministry of Transport still controlled all expenditure on the railways, and in June 1920 it gave permission for the building of six 4 – 6 – 4 tank locomotives. The design had already been prepared and tenders were invited. It now became obvious how expensive each locomotive was going to be, and some haggling went on. Eventually the North British Locomotive Company's bid was accepted, and the firm agreed to build 'six tank engines of the two-cylinder Baltic type at £16,125 each'. Some members of the Board were alarmed at the price and suggested only four should be built, but eventually the original decision was confirmed.

The six engines were delivered from the makers in April 1922. Nothing like them had ever been seen North of the Border before. The first thing to strike the observer about them was their sheer size; each one weighed slightly under 100 tons. In appearance, too, they were unusual. While liveried for the most part in the usual dark green lined out in white and black, with crimson lake framing and black smokebox and cylinder covers, the boiler cladding of smooth rolled steel plating was left unpainted but burnished to give a metallic blue appearance. The outer dome-cover was flat-topped; the three-safety valves and whistle were housed together in a casing above the firebox. The smokebox door bulged forwards to resemble a shallow dome turned on its side and the handrail attached to its door formed a complete ring. The side tanks extended forwards as far as the front coupled axle, and above them, as in the LTSR Baltics, were long box-shaped containers to hold the fire-irons. In front of each a half-splasher over the leading coupled wheel was continued further forwards to cover the piston valve and forward parts of the Walschaert's valve gear. The front and rear bogies, which were identical, had separate splashers over each wheel. (No subsequent locomotive built for a British railway was given these embellishments). The huge cylinders, as large as those of the Brighton 4 – 6 – 4s, were set at an almost undiscernible angle (1 in 75) to the horizontal, and had prominent tail rods. On each tank side the locomotive's number appeared *above* the Company's initials. The downward-projecting life guards at either side at each end of the framing had their edges at an angle

forwards from the buffer beam, as on the LTSR Baltics.

Internally, too, there were unusual features not immediately visible from without. The large and roomy cab, with two windows on either side, was arranged for right-hand driving, but the regulator, brake and whistle control handles were double, three shafts going laterally across the face-plate of the firebox, with handles at either end. The firehole door opened inwards, the opening itself being twenty inches in diameter; it had no outer protective flap, so the footplate could become extremely warm -which in Scottish climatic conditions would seldom be an occasion for complaint. There were bench seats on either side beneath the windows. Other unusual features were roller bearings for the return cranks of the valve gear and a steam-operated motor

placed just in front of the leading coupled wheel's axle between the frames, to actuate the reversing gear. The main frames had to be cranked slightly inwards by their own thickness to allow room for the 22-inch cylinders. A Robinson-type superheater with 21 elements provided superheat up to 330 degrees Centigrade. Coil springs supported the bogie wheels, laminated springs the coupled wheels. Water-storage was provided in a space beneath the coal bunker as well as in the side tanks. The smokebox contained an ash-ejector, and provision was made to keep any coal dust from depositing itself within the cab by means of a water-sprinkler system.

The engines, numbered 540 – 545, were a considerable advertisement for the Company, press publicity ensuring that in their early days crowds would gather

Below: 4 – 6 – 4 No. 543 soon after completion, about to leave St. Enoch, Glasgow, on a train for the coast.

National Railway Museum

WHITELEGG'S IMPRESSIVE 2 CYLINDER 4–6–4T FOR THE GLASGOW AND SOUTH WESTERN RAILWAY BY THE NORTH BRITISH LOCOMOTIVE COMPANY IN 1922

at suitable vantage points to see them go by. Three were shedded at Ayr to do a double Glasgow-and-back turn each day; two others went to Corkerhill to cover Clyde Coast diagrams; one was stationed at Hurlford to work Carlisle expresses over the steeply-graded 24-mile Glasgow-Kilmarnock section, again doing two double journeys daily. Thus the engines were not exactly over-worked; those based at Ayr having 165 miles to cover each day, those at Corkerhill much less, and those at Hurlford only 100 miles or so.

Above: No. 15400, less than four months before withdrawal from service, and in rather dirty condition, moves into a siding at Ayr after detachment from a train from Glasgow, in September 1934.
E.R. Morten

Right: 4-6-4 No. 15401 (formerly G&SWR No. 541), awaiting duty after coaling-up. Note the height of the coal in the bunker. *Photomatic*

Left: 4–6–4 No. 15403 (formerly G&SWR No. 543) in LMS black livery in the thirties. Note that the formerly prominent cylinder tail rods have been considerably shortened.
National Railway Museum

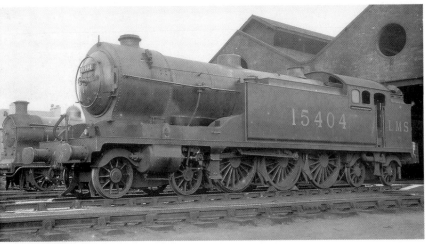

Left: No. 15404 outside (Corkerhill?) shed. Note the apparent absence of a whistle; this in fact was incorporated with the three safety valves inside the casing above the firebox; also the rather unusual bend in the boiler hand-rail to avoid the clack-box.
P.J. Hughes Collection

Below: Towards the end of its working life No. 15405 moves back to take over an afternoon train from Glasgow St. Enoch in April 1933. *E.R. Morten*

Soon after its construction No. 544 was given a test run over the whole of the main line to Carlisle. Although it was not intended to use this type south of Kilmarnock Whitelegg was thinking ahead and wished to find out if the use of a more powerful locomotive than those then available could eliminate piloting. As things stood there were rigid load limitations applicable to the only 4 – 6 – 0s the GSWR then had, those built by James Mason in 1903, whose nominal tractive effort was 20,400 lb, and it is significant that even when they first came out and loads were somewhat lighter than in the early 'twenties, Charles Rous-Marten, who was keen to assess their abilities, had considerable difficulty in finding a train headed by one of them which did not also require piloting south of Kilmarnock; even when first built they were really too small for the job in hand. The new 4 – 6 – 4s with their larger boilers and cylinders, working at the same steam pressure but with the advantage of high superheat, could surely be expected to do better than the older engines, and point the way to a new design of six-coupled engines which might eliminate piloting altogether.

The results of the test runs, were published in *The Locomotive* and the table below was compiled from that article. (In the latter passing and arrival times were sometimes shown to the nearest quarter-minute and sometimes in decimals of a minute; I have modified these to show them in minutes and seconds and they may not always be precisely correct). The tests, one in either direction, certainly showed that the schedules then ruling on the GSWR main line to Carlisle could be kept with loads between 80 and 105 tons beyond the existing limits. An average coal consumption of 0.166 lb per ton mile, however, seems excessive. In 1910 a new superheated Dunalastair IV in coal trials on the CR main line between Perth and Carlisle, a more difficult road than that traversed by No. 544, achieved an average figure of 0.106 lb per ton-mile.

These locomotives experienced the 'teething troubles' usual when a new design is put on the road for the first time. There was a good deal of trouble at first with hot boxes on the bogies, which was eventually put right. Steam from the chimney tended to beat down across the tops of the tanks and obscure the forward view – something that could probably have been cured by fitting deflector plates, but these devices were still some years away in the future. Most significant of all, from the point of view of safety, was a tendency to roll violently on imperfect patches of track -a fault which, as has already been seen, plagued the first LBSCR 4 – 6 – 4 and caused two derailments, and was to show itself again in 1927 with the Southern Railway's 2 – 6 – 4 'River' tank engines, culminating in the fatal accident at Sevenoaks which caused them to be withdrawn and converted into tender locomotives.

TEST RUN FROM GLASGOW TO CARLISLE & BACK:

Date of Test: 4th May 1922.
Locomotive: 4 – 6 – 4T No. 544.
Load: Outwood journey: 310 tons to Kilmarnock, 340 tons thence to Dumfries, 440 tons onwards to Carlisle.
Return journey: 440 tons to Dumfries, 325 tons thence to Kilmarnock: 360 tons onwards to Glasgow.

Outward journey:			*Return journey:*	
Miles:	m. s.		*Miles:*	m. s.
0.0 Glasgow (St. Enoch)	00 00		0.0 Carlisle	00 00
4.4 Kennishead	08 12		8.8 Gretna Jn.	12 15
7.5 Barrhead	12 00		17.8 Annan	23 57
14.3 Lugton	24 45		24.7 Ruthwell	31 33
16.7 Dunlop	27 30		33.2 Dumfries	41 30
	sigs.		0.0 Dumfries	00 00
24.5 Killmarnock	36 10		3.6 Holywood	06 19
0.0 Kilmarnock	00 00		7.4 Auldgirth	11 19
1.7 Hurlford	03 50		11.3 Closeburn	16 08
9.2 Mauchline	16 13		14.3 Thornhill	19 53
21.0 New Cumnock	30 15		17.6 Carronbridge	24 57
40.4 Carronbridge	51 15		Signal stop	
54.4 Holywood	64 45		26.1 Sanquhar	42 15
	sigs.		29.6 Kirkconnel	47 04
58.0 Dumfries	69 34		37.0 New Cumnock	55 04
0.0 Dumfries	00 00		Signal stop	
8.5 Ruthwell	13 06		58.0 Kilmarnock	73 09
15.4 Annan	20 21		0.0 Kilmarnock	00 00
24.4 Gretna Jn.	29 36		7.8 Dunlop	15 30
33.2 Carlisle	40 36		17.0 Barrhead	26 46
			24.5 Glasgow (St. Enoch)	37 21

In his 'Locomotive Practice and Performance' articles in the *Railway Magazine* Cecil J Allen gave a number of examples of the work of these engines in daily service. One was over the heavily-graded line from St. Enoch to Kilmarnock, when the driver considered that a 375-ton load was too heavy to tackle unaided and so was given a 4 – 4 – 0 as pilot. The two engines kept time on the 35-minute schedule, with a minimum of 35 m.p.h. on Neilston bank and nothing more than 62½ on the subsequent descent; the run therefore lacked any indication of the 4 – 6 – 4's capabilities. On the Glasgow to Ayr expresses he gave details of runs in both directions, mostly on the 50-minute non-stop trains, which were set out in the table below. The line is easily graded, gently rising as far as Howwood, gently falling thence to Bogside, and level from there almost the whole way to Ayr.

The first three journeys were all made behind No. 540. The loads on the first two were light, and time was gained in one case without any great effort, but lost in the other through excessive caution after passing Beith; the minimum in both cases was 50 m.p.h. at Howwood, and nothing higher than 62½ was touched beyond. On the third run the extra 110 tons of train gave the engine a little more to do; as far as Prestwick the running was very similar to that on the first occasion, despite the fact that the load was half as much again; speeds varied between 55 and 64 m.p.h. the whole way from Elderslie to slowing down for the slack beyond Prestwick. None of these runs was impressive, but an impressive performance was not called for.

A year and a half later Allen noted a rather better achievement, also on a 50-minute Ayr express, with No. 541, which gained 1¼ minutes on schedule despite two slight signal checks, hauling a 230-ton load; maximum speeds were 68 at Glengarnock and near Kilwinning and 69 at Bogside. A few years later, shortly before these engines were displaced from this particular service, he published two logs from the railway writer David Smith, which are interesting in the comparison they give between the 4 – 6 – 4s and the smaller 4 – 4 – 0 type which was to succeed it. No. 15401 (formerly No. 541) was delayed by signals before stopping at Paisley, but then covered the 33.7 miles to Ayr without any checks in 37¾ minutes with the comparatively heavy load of 345 tons, attaining 51 m.p.h. at Howwood and gradually rising to 64 at Bogside, and continuing at the mile-a-minute rate until slowing down for Ayr, thus more than regaining the lost time. This was, as Allen remarked, 'a fine piece of work', but the effort of the new Class 2P 4 – 4 – 0 was more interesting; with a 280-ton load it gained 1¼ minutes on the 50-minute schedule, reaching 52 m.p.h. at Howwood, 60 at Dalry and continuing at over mile-a-minute rate until being eased at Barassie. Although the Class 2Ps were so much smaller and less powerful than the Baltics they were well able to manage these trains with loads approaching 300 tons, and eventually they displaced the big tanks altogether.

Despite the potential power of these monsters it would seem that they were never called upon to display it to the full. The easy 50-minute non-stop schedule between Glasgow and Ayr was never reduced while they were in charge of these expresses, and no attempt seems ever to have been made to see by how much it might be cut. One would have thought that a five-minute quickening would have been feasible. No speed higher than 69 mph was ever attributed to them on this easy road, where they might have been expected to match the contemporary performances of the LBSCR Baltics. Had Whitelegg remained charge of the locomotive department he would surely have seen to it that their

LOGS OF JOURNEYS BETWEEN GLASGOW & AYR: 1922 – 1929:

Locomotive No:	540	540	540	541	15401	595*
Gross load in tons:	210	210	320	230	345	280
Miles	m. s.	m. s.	m. s.	m. s.	m. s.	m. s.
0.0 Glasgow (St. Enoch)	00 00	00 00	00 00	00 00	00 00	00 00
1.6 Shields Rd.	04 05	04 00	04 30		04 29	04 15
4.2 Cardonald	07 25	07 15	07 50		08 14 sigs.	07 50
7.7 Paisley	11 40	11 15	12 00	11 00	14 37	12 05
9.7 Elderslie	14 20	13 55	14 50	13 33	04 18	14 35
13.8 Howwood	19 10	18 55	19 50	18 28	09 04	19 20
16.5 Lochside				21 28	12 07	22 25
18.6 Beith	24 30	24 10	25 15	23 35		
20.6 Glengarnock					16 26	26 45
23.3 Dalry	29 35	29 35	30 10	28 03	19 10	29 30
26.8 Kilwinning	33 10	33 15	33 50	31 18	22 37	33 00
30.2 Irvine	36 35	36 55	37 10	34 18	25 54	36 10
34.9 Troon	41 35	42 30	41 50	sigs.	30 42	40 50
38.3 Prestwick	45 05	46 15	45 20	42 28	34 06	44 35
			PWS			
40.2 Newton-on-Ayr	47 00	48 20	48 15		36 03	46 45
41.4 Ayr	49 05	50 15	50 15	46 48	37 48	48 45

*4 – 4 – 0 Class 2P.

potential was better exploited. However, after the merging of the GSWR with other lines into the London Midland & Scottish Railway the initiative passed from Kilmarnock and the Derby traditions took over. There was no enthusiasm on the part of the LMSR authorities for such huge machines; they were still multiplying their 3-cylinder 4 – 4 – 0 compounds and 2-cylinder Class 2P 4 – 4 – 0s as the answer to all passenger haulage problems except the heaviest Scottish trains. There was also the question of whether these large tank engines could be safely used at all, which was highlighted by the Sevenoaks accident in August 1927. If smaller and

lighter engines, which had the advantage of being standard types, could do the work the 4 – 6 – 4s had been built to do, where was the point of keeping the latter at all?

So the éclat with which the Baltics had been greeted in 1922 was short-lived, and the sweet beginning had a sour ending. First the beautiful livery disappeared, and was replaced by Midland red; then that in turn gave place to black, a premonition of the doom awaiting them, for all were withdrawn between 1935 and 1936 after an active life shorter then even their LTSR cousins had enjoyed.

7. HUGHES'S BALTICS FOR THE EX-L&Y ROUTES OUT OF MANCHESTER

The last 4 – 6 – 4 tank locomotive type to be built in Great Britain, and also the largest, appeared on the LMSR in 1924, while G Hughes was still Chief Mechanical Engineer of that railway. He had been in charge of the Locomotive Department on the Lancashire & Yorkshire Railway from his appointment in 1904 until the time when it amalgamated with the LNWR at the beginning of 1922, a year before the general amalgamations of 1923 and enjoyed a considerable reputation as a skilful and forward-looking locomotive engineer when his first 4 – 6 – 0 passenger locomotives took the rails of 1907. However, their poor performances were to call his ability into question, for this type turned out to be an unexpected and abject failure in traffic. It was impressive enough to look at, with its large boiler and nominal tractive effort greater than that of any other British express locomotive at the time of its appearance, but it had some fatal flaws at its front end, such as restricted steam passages and slide valves instead of piston valves, and simply would not run freely; footplate crews disliked these engines and they were very heavy on coal. So they did not last long in their original state, but were withdrawn from service at the end of the First World War and were lucky to last that long.

However, though he had got off on the wrong foot with his first attempt at building a 4 – 6 – 0, Hughes did much better the second time. During 1920 – 1921 he rebuilt fifteen of the withdrawn engines, making significant alterations, and then built new a further fifty on the same pattern. Of the same general dimensions as their unlucky predecessors, and only two tons heavier, they were much more up-to-date in regard to their front ends. Most importantly, they were superheated; Hughes employed his own patent method, different from all existing methods of superheating. There were as many as 28 elements, which were positioned vertically down either side of the boiler; the cast-iron header which received the saturated steam was above these, in the smokebox, and the similar header which received the superheater steam was below, bolted to the cylinder castings, so that no intermediate steam pipes were required, and the saturated steam could not cool the superheated steam through being in close proximity to it. It was claimed for this design that it resulted in a more even distribution of temperature in the tubes, so that leaks occurred less frequently.

These locomotives also had piston valves in place of slide valves, with a separate Walschaert's gear working each one, whereas the unrebuilt engines had Joy's valve gear placed interiorly and working the outside valves through rocking bars. They also had mechanical lubrication, as always with superheated engines. In addition they were fitted with Hughes' patent 'ball release valves', which were intended to relieve compression within the cylinders if necessary while steam was being applied, lessen the pressure of air in front of the moving pistons when steam had been shut off, and prevent the accumulation of condensed water in the cylinders. They did this automatically by connecting the cylinder interiors with the steam chests as soon as the pressure in the former became greater than in the latter. Similar valves, similarly placed, were fitted to the two outside cylinders of the Horwich-built 'Crab' 2 – 6 – 0s produced by Fowler after Hughes' retirement, but were not used by any other engines on the LMSR. Externally the rebuilds were distinguished from their predecessors by the raised running plate and external steam pipe on either side of the smokebox, by the visible external valve gear and by the fact that the piston valves above the cylinders, and also by having a much larger cab.

These locomotives were a great improvement on the former unrebuilt ones, and Hughes envisaged them taking the places of the ex-LNWR 4 – 6 – 0 engines on the heavier West Coast expresses between Crewe and Carlisle. However, they had not been designed for long-distance traffic, and when so employed did not prove entirely suitable, so that after Hughes had retired Sir Henry Fowler, his successor and former head of the Locomotive Department on the MR, after greatly multiplying the numbers of the three-cylinder 4 – 4 – 0 compounds which had been built by R.M. Deeley for that railway, began to think in terms of much larger engines, the end consequence being the building of the 'Royal Scots'. In the meantime the Horwich-built 4 – 6 – 0s supplemented the 'Claughton' and 'Prince of Wales' types on the main line across Shap, and a tank engine version of the former was decided upon to cope with the haulage of heavy suburban trains on the branches which radiated from Manchester and also of the Manchester to Blackpool and Southport expresses – this locomotive being the subject of this chapter.

Fifty such tank engines were originally intended and thirty were begun, but only ten were actually completed. There was a change of plan and the partly-finished thirty were reconstructed as 4 – 6 – 0s. By the time the ten were completed the LYR and the LNWR, already united into one company, had been merged into the new LMSR group, so that they received the latter's crimson lake livery from the start. Except for their extended frames, rear bogies, closed-in cabs and coal bunkers, and their short-side tanks (which only reached as far as the rear end of the dome) they were the same as the rebuilt 4—6—0s.

These engines were larger than any other tank locomotives previously built for service in this country.

and unique in being four-cylindered. They were also the only tank engines which, so far as their mechanisms were concerned, were exactly similar to an existing express passenger type. When he contemplated their construction Hughes is reported to have been influenced by the example of Whitelegg's GSWR Baltics, and had in mind borrowing one to test it out on the Lancashire services which radiated from Manchester. The routes on which either type operated were comparable in length, though scarcely in difficulty, for the journeys of 35 to 50 miles for which the Hughes engines were intended were not, like those south of the Clyde estuary, level or gently inclined, but included some very tough gradients indeed, such as the banks between Bolton and Accrigton going up to Baxenden summit, which rose by degrees to 1 in 68, or the appalling short pitch of 1 in 40/38 on the same stretch in the reverse direction. The sturdy little 2 – 4 – 2 tank engines built before Hughes' time by Aspinall and Hoy were now finding it difficult to cope with crowded commuter trains, especially over the Accrington and Bury route, and needed replacing by more powerful machines. With a nominal tractive effort one-and-three-quarter times as great as that of the later 2 – 4 – 2s there could be little doubt that the new 4 – 6 – 4s would make adequate replacements – indeed, one wonders if they were not *too*powerful, since they were also very heavy and would have to haul their own extra weight as well as a train of coaches. The Blackpool and Southport trains were on the whole an easier proposition once one was clear of Manchester. Also, there had been an easing of timings during the war. Probably the hardest L&Y train to work had now become the 4.25 p.m. from Salford to Colne, booked non-stop over the 28½ miles to Burnley Barracks in 49 minutes over a road where high speed was impossible because of restriction and with Baxenden summit to be crossed *en route*. In his

articles on locomotive performance in the Railway Magazine, Cecil J Allen more than once enthused over the work of L&Y 2 – 4 – 2 tank engines in this train.

The first Hughes 4 – 6 – 4 had a successful début in March 1924 when, still in workshop grey livery, it had a short trial run and then, three weeks later, on 8th April, was given an official test. According to an anonymous account given in the *Mancunian*, a duplicated magazine published by the Manchester Locomotive Society, in its issue of May 1987,

. . . . . it ran trials between Bolton and Hellifield. Its train consisted of ten bogie coaches and a dynamometer car, a total weight of 304 tons. During the run the engine is reported to have shown up to advantage, negotiating the 6-miles' climb at 1 in 72 and 1 in 74 from Astley Bridge to the Sough tunnel on the outward run in 11 minutes 50 seconds without being pushed in any way. The cut-off was in the region of 35% and the regulator was about half open. On the return journey the 6½ miles from Blackburn to the Sough tunnel was covered in 12 minutes 35 seconds from a standing start at Blackburn, the engine running tender first. Between Newsholme and Hellifield on the outward run a speed of 58 m.p.h. was reached, and it was reported that the engine rode smoothly. In fact, all through the trials it showed remarkable freedom from oscillation and ability to take curves.

Immediately after their construction the LMSR seems to have felt a certain pride in these huge machines, although they were not representative of their practice at the time like the 4 – 4 – 0 three-cylinder compounds of which such large numbers were being built. No. 11114 was sent to be exhibited at the Wembley Exhibition of 1924, where it rubbed shoulders with the more famous LNER *Flying Scotsman* and GWR *Caerphilly Castle*. The

Below: 4 – 6 – 4 No. 11114 posed for official photograph soon after construction. Note the unusual shape of the cab roof and the laterally-placed safety valves.
National Railway Museum

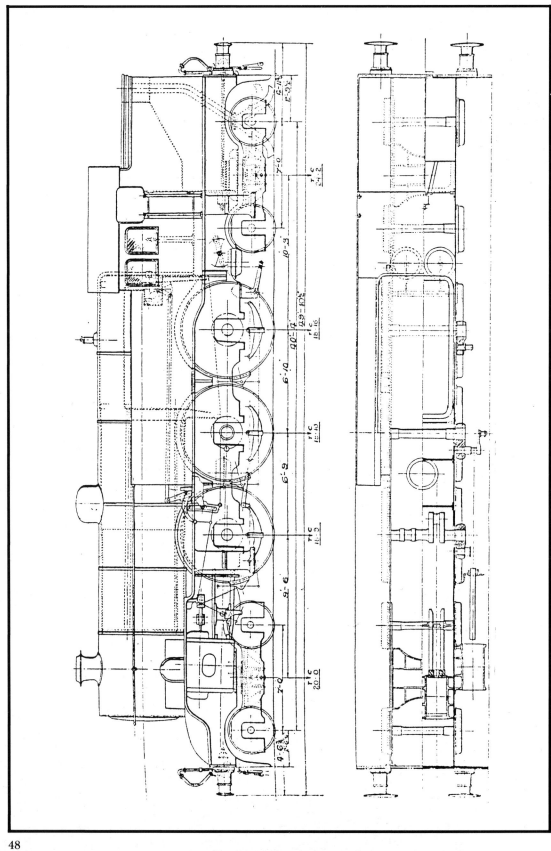

HUGHES'S POWERFUL 4 CYLINDER 4–6–4T BUILT AT HORWICH 1924 FOR THE LMS

following year No. 11112 went in July to take part in the Centenary celebration of the Stockton & Darlington Railway as Exhibit No. 40, and two months later appeared again in the Railway Centenary celebrations at Belle Vue Gardens, Manchester, along with such worthies as the LNER 4 – 6 – 2 *Centenary*, the ancient LNWR single-wheeler *Cornwall* and the even more ancient *Locomotion* No. 1, then exactly 100 years old. This was the only Baltic ever to be publicly exhibited.

The 4 – 6 – 4s were at first used exclusively on the Central Division, the former L&YR, and regularly took turns with the smaller 2 – 4 – 2 tanks on services like the 4.25 p.m. from Salford to Colne, mentioned above. Cecil J Allen timed No. 11110 once on this train when the load was 260 tons, and noticed its superior ability at climbing heavy gradients. Baxenden 20 miles from Salford and only just beyond the summit, was passed in 33 minutes 5 seconds from the start despite a signal check on the 1 in 76 just before Haslingden tunnel which brought the speed down to 26 m.p.h.; the engine then accelerated to 34 through Haslingden station. In consequence the train was 3 minutes early through Accrington, where it slipped some coaches.

During 1926 these locomotives began to find their ways on to other duties, and at the end of the year they were all employed on the Manchester to Buxton services, where they replaced the less powerful ex-LNWR 4 – 6 – 2 tank engines; while here they were occasionally seen at Crewe or Stoke-on-Trent. Early in 1928 Nos. 11115 – 11118 were moved south to work on the outer suburban trains between St. Pancras and Bedford for a short while; they were possibly being tested against

4 – 6 – 4 No. 11112 taking part in the Stockton & Darlington centenary cavalcade in 1925.
C.J. Fryer Collection

4 – 6 – 4 No. 11117 standing at Manchester (Victoria).
C.J. Fryer Collection

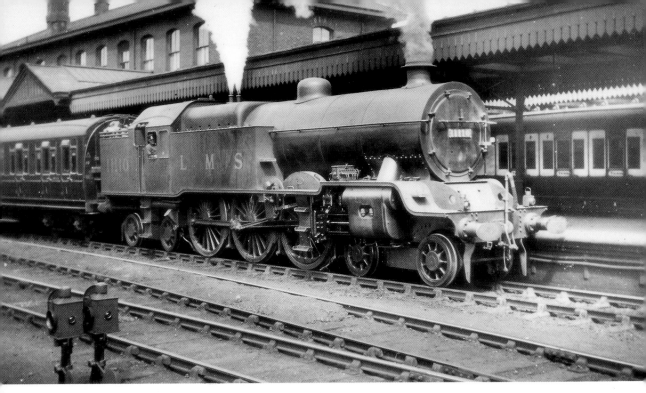

ex-LTSR 4 – 6 – 4s, and did not stay there long, return-ing to the Buxton line before the spring. One would very much like to know how they performed on a line where high downhill speeds were possible, but no records ap-pear to exist. By the end of 1929 they were all back once more on the Central Division, working as before on the Manchester to Blackpool and Southport services and on the trains to Colne.

In 1930 one of them was tested out against the recently-built 2 – 6 – 4 No. 2371, designed by Sir Henry Fowler. This and its sister engines – 125 built in all – were lighter and nominally less powerful than the 4 – 6 – 4s, but it was suspected that they could do the latters' duties equally well, and as it turned out the tests confirmed this belief. Two days, a fortnight apart, were chosen, when a particular sequence of trains was operated, first by the Baltic, then by the 2 – 6 – 4, on 17th July and 31st respectively. The trains were:

　9.00 a.m. express passenger, Manchester (Victoria) to Southport:

　11 a.m. express passenger, Southport to Manchester (Victoria):

　4.25 p.m. express passenger, Salford to Colne:

　6.25 p.m. slow passenger, Colne to Manchester.

Coal was weighed on to the locomotives' bunkers, but it did not prove possible to estimate water consumption accurately. Both locomotives performed equally well in actual running, both on the relatively easy runs to Southport and back and on the harder assignments on the Colne line. However, when coal consumption figures were compared, there could be no question which locomotive had been more economical. The figures in lb per ton-mile, the weights of the locomotives being included in the calculation, were as follows:

Loco.	Journey	lbs. of Coal used per ton-mile
11112	Manchester – Southport – Manchester	0.120
do.	Salford – Colne & Colne – Manchester	0.206
2371	Manchester – Southport – Manchester	0.103
do.	Salford – Colne & Colne – Manchester	0.162

The differences in consumption in the case of each engine for the two routes of course reflect the much heavier graidents on the Colne line.

It was accordingly concluded by the LMSR authorities that the standard 2 – 6 – 4 tank engine was able to take the usual 'Class 4' loading over both routes satisfactori-ly and could replace the 4 – 6 – 4. The significant reduction in coal consumption made it desirable that it should be so used.

The question then arose: what was to be done with these ten locomotives, which were not only provenly heavy on coal but also spent an inordinate time being maintained or repaired? One suggestion was that they should be rebuilt as tender locomotives, but this came to nothing. In 1932 Fowler was succeeded by W.A. Stanier from the GWR as Chief Mechanical Engineer. His first idea was to re-boiler as many existing engines as possible with the new standard tapered boiler, and the Horwich-built 4 – 6 – 4s and 4 – 6 – 0s were includ-ed in those marked out for such treatment. Then follow-ed a much more radical change of plan, when the 'Scrap-and-build' policy was begun, which was eventually to lead to the production of so many of those highly-successful 'maids of all work', the 'Black Five' 4 – 6 – 0s.

Right: No. 11110, the first of the series, at Agecroft shed ahead of what appears to be another of the same type. Note the long shovel on the ground beneath the cab-door – thrown out to cool down? The engine is still, unusually, in LMS red livery. *P.J. Hughes*

Left: No. 11110 heading a Manchester – Buxton train in the thirties. Note the cut-away sides of the buffer beam, done to facilitate platform clearance. The train has halted at Stockport station.

National Railway Museum

Right: No. 11112 at Agecroft shed, Manchester. Note the unusual 3-level step ladder to the cab and running plate and the unusual way in which the opening above the footplate door extends into the cab roof, which latter slopes well down at either side to obtain clearance of the loading gauge. *P.J. Hughes*

So the Hughes engines were doomed. Withdrawals began in 1938 and by the beginning of 1942 the class was extinct. There were then no more Baltics running in Great Britain, apart from the four still at work between Belfast and Bangor. Their day was definitely over.

Can these engines be considered as successes, failures, or somewhat in between? To quote from the already-cited issue of the *Mancunian* again:

Since their withdrawal, opinions have varied amongst writers and enthusiasts about the merits or otherwise of the class. The staff at Agecroft (*a Manchester depot*), which at one time or another had every engine shedded there, seemed to like them. On the other hand, an Accrington driver, writing in *Trains Illustrated* .... said that the men there called them 'Bucking Broncos' because they were top-heavy and rocked a great deal. Yet another driver who had experience of them responded by saying that their unpopularity with engine crews was mainly due to the great height of the tanks, which allowed only a poor view ahead. This gentlemen, also commented on their ability to climb Baxenden bank out of Accrington, and said that if they stalled, it was usually due to the inexperience of the crew. He continued by saying that Blackpool men never stalled the Baltic tanks, and that he had gone up the hill in fine style behind one of them with 9 on, without a banker and with Blackpool men on the footplate ....

It is probably fair to let Eric Mason, one time Shed Master at Agecroft, have the last word. In one of his books he says he was personally concerned with the working of these engines during practically the whole

4 – 6 – 4 No. 11113 under repair at Horwich works. Each of the 16 wire ropes would be carrying a load of over 5½ tons.

National Railway Museum

of their existence, and that for the work for which they were designed they were definitely more than successful. In his opinion the only point in their design which could be criticised was the poor look-out from the footplate, which meant that the drivers had to spend most of their journeys with their heads out of the side windows. But he said there was no question as to their capabilities and capacity for working trains, and that they were smooth easy-riding locos which were used freely on the main line expresses between Manchester and Blackpool, Southport and Yorkshire. He also says he never had a complaint about their rough riding. He accepted, however, that they were not cheap to maintain, and this feature must surely have detracted from the success of the design.

It seems fair to conclude that these last Baltics were good performers which had eventually to give way to better ones that had the advantage of being built in large numbers, so that spares were readily obtainable, and which were less costly to maintain. But it does seem a pity that not one member of this ultimate among British tank locomotive types was selected for preservation. They represented a peak of achievement, even if only in sheer size and weight, being one hundredweight short of the 100-ton mark when in working order · and indeed topped that level when the driver and fireman were both on the footplate.

8.COMMENTS AND CONCLUSIONS

The dinosaurs, those celebrated giants who could not adapt to a changed environment, were reproducing themselves over hundreds of centuries; the Baltic tanks, giants of the railways, were produced for only about twelve years. Were they, too, metaphorically dinosaurs? Why did the 4 – 6 – 4 type fail to catch on?

On the face of it they had plenty going for them. The provision of a rear bogie allowed the inclusion of a really sizeable coal bunker with space for water beneath, and there was plenty of room for a large cab. The difficulty of making long non-stop runs could to some extent have been overcome by the provision of a water-scoop on lines which had troughs. There was a saving in weight illustrated by the difference between the Hughes 4 – 6 – 0 tender locomotive and its tank engine counterpart – some 12 tons even though the tender was a rather small one. A tank locomotive with a bogie at each end could run as smoothly backwards as forwards, and did not necessarily have to be turned at the end of each journey.

Nevertheless it was the 2 – 6 – 4, not the 4 – 6 – 4 wheel arrangement which proved more attractive as a type for building in large numbers with standardized parts, so far as the LMSR was concerned, this being the system which absorbed four of the companies which had built Baltics, while on the SR a lighter 2 – 6 – 4 had shown itself to be as good as, if not slightly better than the Brighton 4 – 6 – 4s in hauling the chief trains on the Central Section (though that particular class was also more prone to oscillation at speed, and after the Sevenoaks accident had to be reconstructed as tender locomotives). In Ulster, too, 2 – 6 – 4 tanks of the Ulster Transport Authority showed themselves better than the BCDR Baltics both in performance and economy. All the 4 – 6 – 4 Classes dealt with in this book were perhaps a shade too large for the work they had to do. This was above all true of those on the GSWR, where they were put on duties which Class 2P 4 – 4 – 0s later showed they could manage perfectly well – and they, though they had tenders attached, were four tons lighter than the tanks they replaced.

It could be said, perhaps with a little exaggeration, that each of the Baltic designs except Crosthwait's was one man's pet idea which did not commend itself to those who came after him. The consequence was that no trend was established. Another noticeable thing was that, except on the BCDR, the designer did not remain in his superintendency long after his type had been built. Robert Whitelegg had been given notice to leave even before his LTSR Baltics had been completed. Lawson Billinton, though he tested and modified two of his 4 – 6 – 4s over several years, did not venture to multiply their numbers until shortly before the railway company he served was absorbed in the SR; he then chose to retire. Rutherford was in the same position on

the FR, and Whitelegg for a second time on the GSWR, when both companies were submerged in the LMSR system and Barrow and Kilmarnock had to give place to Derby. When be built his ten Baltics, Hughes was on the point of retirement. The Chief Mechanical Engineers who assumed control of the amalgamated lines, each found himself holding a baby he had not fathered, and an enormous baby too, with which he did not really know what to do. Only Crosthwait remained as head of his locomotive department on the BCDR for many years after the Baltics he had ordered were delivered. How much he was responsible for their design is a matter of opinion, but it is significant, perhaps, that he did not have any more constructed, but reverted to the 4 – 4 – 2 type when the next batch of new engines for this line was needed.

One observes, too, that each of the six types except the Brighton 4 – 6 – 4 was unsteady at a speed, at any rate according to some of those who handled them, and the Brighton tanks were only steady after repeated derailments had obliged them to undergo some drastic reconstruction. If after 1924 any Chief Mechanical Engineer had been thinking of building express tank locomotives, the accident at Sevenoaks in August 1927 would surely have deterred him. It was not so much that a six-coupled engine with large sides was unsafe in itself, but that when it came to a bad patch of road it reacted more completely to it, rolling with greater amplitude and for a longer time. No Chief Mechanical Engineer could be sure that this would never happen, since a prolonged spell of wet weather could affect the foundations of the permanent way quite suddenly and unexpectedly – as was the case at Sevenoaks. It was safer to build engines with tenders, which could steady them from behind. A few extra tons' weight was a small matter when safety was at stake.

Then there was the matter of costliness of maintenance. In the case of the Hughes Baltics, this was largely because they had four cylinders, two of which, in Maunsell's phrase, were relatively un-get-at-able. The Furness engines too, being inside-cylindered, needed more time for maintenance. The other four types were all two-cylinder locomotives whose moving parts were more easily got at. If one of these six types had been built in really large numbers, with spare parts kept in store, maintenance costs would no doubt have been much less.

There is also the consideration that while these six Baltic types were made specifically to be used in certain limited areas, the 1923 groupings obliterated the smaller companies which served comparatively small areas. Locomotive designers had now to think of the needs of systems which extended from London to the extremities of the United Kingdom. A type which could go almost anywhere and do almost anything was the ideal. Stanier acheived it with his 'Black Fives', Collett with his 'Halls', Maunsell (almost7 with his N and U class 2—6—0s. These were all tender locomotives, but the weight of the tender added to that of the engine was not a fixed quantity; one could fit a smaller tender where a large one was not necessary, and the total tonnage might not be so very much greater than that of a tank engine of comparable power. It was more important that the water tanks should not run dry on a long run, than that a pound or so of coal should be saved for each mile run.

So the building of all these Baltics, seen with the advantages of hindsight, was probably a mistake. They were the productions of engineers who had to consider the needs of a limited system, and they tried to build horses for courses. Probably it would have been better if some of them had been designed with tenders in the first place (though this comment could scarcely apply to the LTSR and BCDR engines, since both these companies used only tank engines for their passenger traffic). It is noticeable that when British Railways brought out its range of standard locomotives no express passenger tank design was included.

One cannot regret the Baltics; they added variety to locomotive scene and, in their original forms and liveries, some of them were real eye-catchers so far as appearance went. But they and their times were mutually out of joint. They had no future and did not lead anywhere; they were not parts of changing continuity of design but a blind alley. So perhaps they *were* dinosaurs. One wishes they had attracted train-timing enthusiasts more than they did. Fortunately they did attract photographers, as the illustrations in this book show.

BRITISH 4 – 6 – 4 TANK LOCOMOTIVES: DIMENSIONS AND DETAILS

Railway company	LT&SR	LB&SCR	B&CDR	F.R.	G&SWR	LM&SR
Loco superintendent/C.M.E.	R. Whitelegg	L. Billinton	J. Crosthwait	D. Rutherford	R. Whitelegg	G. Hughes
Nos constructed	8	7	4	5	6	10
Nos given	2100 – 07	327 – 333	22 – 25	115 – 119	540 – 545	11110 – 9
Date first locomotive completed	12/1912	3/1914	1/1920	11/1920	4/1922	3/1924
Wheel diameter (coupled)	6' 3"	6' 9"	5' 6"	5' 8"	6' 0"	6' 3"
Wheel diameter (bogie)	3' 1"	3' 6"	3' 0"	3' 2"	3' 6"	3' 0½"
Coupled wheelbase	13' 10"	14' 9"	12' 2"	13' 3"	13' 2"	13' 7"
Total wheelbase	38' 10½"		35' 3"		39' 0"	40' 4"
Cylinders	(2) 20" x 26"	(2) 22" x 28"	(2) 19" x 26"	(2) 19½" x 26"	(2) 22" x 26"	(4) 16½" x 26"
Valve gear	Walschaert's	Walschaert's	Walschaert's	Stephenson's	Walschaert's	Walschaert's
Boiler length	14' 11¼"	15' 5"	12' 11"	15' 0"	14' 11"	15' 0"
Boiler diameter	5' 0"	5' 5"	5' 0"	5' 0"	5' 6¼"	5' 8¼"
Heating surface: tubes & firebox	1,296 sq ft	1,687 sq ft	1,622 sq ft	2,003 sq ft	1,730 sq ft	1,997 sq ft
superheater	319 sq ft	383 sq ft			255 sq ft	430 sq ft
Grate Area (sq ft)	24.9	26.7	24.7	26.0	30	29.6
Tractive effort (85% wkg pressure)	21,220 lbf	28,740 lbf	19,340 lbf	21,006 lbf	26,741 lbf	28,879 lbf
Weight in working order	95 t 3 cwt	99 t 0 cwt	81 t 12 cwt	188 t 15 cwt	96 t 7 cwt	99 t 19 cwt
Weight for adhesion	52 t 15 cwt	57 t 1 cwt		55 t 8 cwt	54 t 0 cwt	56 t 10 cwt
Coal capacity	3 tons	3½ tons	4 tons	4 tons	3½ tons	3½ tons
Water capacity	2,200 gall	2,686 gall	2,000 gall	2,200 gall	2,400 gall	2,000 gall

CHANGE OF ADDRESS

Please note that because the cover of this book was printed in advance of the rest of the book that we have since changed our address. The address shown on the inside back cover is therefore incorrect. Please note therefore that all mail orders should be addressed to:

Mail Order Department,
Platform 5 Publishing Ltd.,
Wyvern House,
Old Forge Business Park,
Sark Road,
SHEFFIELD, S2 4HG.

SPECIAL OFFERS

THE HANDBOOK OF BRITISH RAILWAYS STEAM MOTIVE POWER DEPOTS

This four volume series contrives to fill a major gap in published literature by identifying, and pinpointing by means of maps, all 666 depots used throughout the era of BR steam locomotion. Most depots are illustrated with photographs. All books are 273 x 216 mm thread sewn with colour cover. The four volumes are:

Volume 1 – Southern England (includes introduction to series).......(was £7.95) Now £3.95
Volume 2 – Central England, East Anglia and Wales................(was £8.95) Now £3.95
Volume 3 – North Midlands, Lancashire and Yorkshire.............(was £8.95) Now £3.95
Volume 4 – Northern England, Scotland plus index to series........(was £9.95) Now £3.95

ALONG LMS ROUTES

by Bill Hudson (Headstock Publications)

Volume 1 – Central and Western Divisions.

This book takes as its theme a series of journeys illustrated profusely by excellent photographs taken throughot the steam era from pre-grouping days to nationalisation. The author sees railways as part of the environment, and the text and photographs have therefore been selected for interest in the surroundings as well as the trains themselves. 144 pages, Casebound. 273 x 216 mm.(was £14.95) Now £6.95.

The postage and packing charge on these special offer books is 10% (UK) and 20% (overseas) of the **original price.**